The **Mini Rough Guide** to
BARCELONA

ROUGH GUIDES

YOUR TAILOR-MADE TRIP
STARTS HERE

Tailor-made trips and unique adventures crafted by local experts

HOW ROUGHGUIDES.COM/TRIPS WORKS

STEP 1

Pick your dream destination, tell us what you want and submit an enquiry.

STEP 2

Fill in a short form to tell your local expert about your dream trip and preferences.

STEP 3

Our local expert will craft your tailor-made itinerary. You'll be able to tweak and refine it until you're completely satisfied.

STEP 4

Book online with ease, pack your bags and enjoy the trip! Our local expert will be on hand 24/7 while you're on the road.

PLAN AND BOOK YOUR TRIP AT
ROUGHGUIDES.COM/TRIPS

How to download your Free eBook

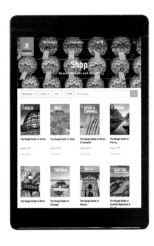

1. Visit **www.roughguides.com/ free-ebook** or scan the **QR code** opposite

2. Enter the code **barcelona634**

3. Follow the simple step-by-step instructions

For troubleshooting contact: mail@roughguides.com

Contents

Introduction

Barcelona may be the second city of Spain, locked in eternal rivalry with Madrid, but it ruled an empire long before Spain was even born. Some two thousand years ago, the Romans, on their way to conquering the whole of Iberia, built a forbidding wall around their settlement on the Mediterranean coast and called it Barcino. Although a visitor could spend days wandering the Barri Gòtic (Gothic Quarter), an atmospheric tangle of medieval buildings and alleyways where the city's glorious past is palpable, Barcelona is more than a living museum. It is a dynamic, creative and daringly modern metropolis.

La Rambla thrums with life night and day

Once a grey industrial port, Barcelona has reinvented itself. Rundown neighbourhoods were revived, numerous urban spaces filled with sculpture and greenery created. The airport, railway and metro have been brought up to date, and new hotels, museums and concert halls have sprung up. The most important physical change, though, has been Barcelona's reorientation towards the sea. With a dynamic port that is now one of the busiest cruise-ship stops in Europe, the Port Olímpic, a further leisure port at Diagonal Mar, its clean beaches and renowned

WHAT'S NEW

Barcelona buzzes with an unstoppable creative energy that shows no sign of letting up. Contemporary additions include Casa Seat (Passeig de Gràcia 109, see page 63), an achingly cool cultural hub that hosts exhibitions and concerts. One of Barcelona's most iconic buildings, the iridescent, pickle-shaped skyscraper Torre Glòries (see page 82), formerly Torre Agbar, has had a spruce-up, offering a brand-new observation deck with panoramic views. For the more intrepid, there's a giant climbing frame suspended in the air by six kilometres (3.7 miles) of tensioned cable – cushions are spread out sporadically, so you can stop mid-climb to savour the view. Adding yet another string to its bow of independent art galleries, Moco Museum (see page 54) has refashioned a sixteenth-century palace into a calming all-white space in busy Barri Gòtic. Although compact, this private collection packs museum-quality art (Keith Haring, Banksy) with intriguing one-off exhibitions on digital and celebrity culture alongside the icons. One of the most anticipated reopenings of the past few years, the refreshed Casa-Museu Gaudí in Park Güell provides a brilliant context to Barcelona's architectural mastermind (see page 69). Another keenly anticipated reopening, Mercat de Sant Antoni (Carrer del Comte d'Urgell 1) is back in business – nine years and an €80m refurbishment later. A gorgeous Art Nouveau mega-market in El Eixample, with an octagonal roof of terracotta and steel, this is where you'll find the freshest, most affordable cuts of cured meat, alongside mountains of olives and vibrant fresh fruit and veg. On Sunday, it transforms into Spain's largest open-air book market.

seafront neighbourhoods, the Catalan capital has succeeded in marrying the pleasures of the Mediterranean with the sophisticated, creative energy of modern Europe. The focus is now on the two main arteries running east–west to the sea, Avinguda Diagonal and Avinguda Paral·lel. The aim is to create a connection between these two roads and the flourishing port with its cruise-ship terminal, and the Forum's trade fair, exhibition and conference venues.

WHEN TO GO

Barcelona is a hugely popular year-round city-break destination. Seasonal attractions range from summer music festivals to Christmas markets. In terms of the weather, the best times to visit are late spring and early autumn, when it's comfortably warm (around 21–25°C) and walking the streets isn't a slog. Evenings might see a chill in the air, but Barcelona in these seasons is often nigh on perfect. However, in summer the city can be unbearably hot and humid, with temperatures averaging 28°C but often climbing much higher. Avoid August, especially, when the climate is at its most unwelcoming and local inhabitants escape the city in droves, leaving many shops, bars and restaurants closed. It's worth considering a winter break, as long as you don't mind the prospect of occasional rain. Even in December, when temperatures hover around 13°C, it's generally still pleasant enough to sit out at a café.

CATALAN CULTURE

Barcelona's physical transformation has accompanied a renaissance of Catalan culture, long marginalised – often overtly repressed – by Spanish rulers. The most ruthless aggression came during the Franco dictatorship, which lasted from the Spanish Civil War of 1936–39 until the dictator's death in 1975. Under the 1979 Statute of Autonomy, Catalonia regained a substantial measure of self-government. Regardless of the political winds, Catalan arts, literature and language are vigorously promoted by the Catalan government.

Reawakened, too, is the pride locals take in their city. The man behind much of its extraordinary architecture is

NOTES

To quickly get the full measure of this dynamic city, hop on (and off wherever you want) the Bus Turístic, or sign up for a walking, bike, boat or scooter tour. Check www.barcelonaturisme. com for the latest offers.

the city's most famous son, Antoni Gaudí (1852–1926), one of the creators of *modernisme*, or Catalan Art Nouveau. Gaudí's buildings still startle: his soaring, unfinished cathedral, La Sagrada Família, is his best-known work, but there are scores more in Barcelona. Around the turn of the twentieth century, a group of *modernistas*, including Lluís Domènech i Montaner and Josep Puig i Cadafalch, dreamed up the most fanciful buildings their rich imaginations and equally rich patrons would allow.

More recent trailblazers include Oriol Bohigas, Enric Ruiz-Geli, Miralles and Tagliabue and a host of international architects like Jean Nouvel, Norman Foster, Richard Rogers, Frank Gehry, Herzog and de Meuron, who have all created new landmarks in the city or have work in progress.

Barcelona has an excellent infrastructure for cyclists

SARDANES

The city – and the region – takes its culture seriously. Rituals like the *sardana*, a traditional dance performed on Saturday evening and Sunday morning in front of the cathedral, and in Plaça Sant Jaume on some Sunday evenings, are held almost sacred. Men, women and children hold hands and form a circle to perform the seemingly simple but highly regimented steps. The band, called a *cobla*, comprising strings, brass and a drum, plays lilting, melancholic tunes as more and more circles form until the entire area is filled with dancers.

DESIGN AND INDUSTRY

Barcelona also nurtured the careers of some of the twentieth-century's greatest artists – the Catalans Joan Miró and Salvador Dalí, and also Pablo Picasso, who spent his formative years in the city before seeking fame in Paris (Barcelona's Museu Picasso has the largest collection of his work outside Paris). Few other cities are as invested in innovation and creativity as Barcelona. The opening of every ahead-of-the-curve museum, bridge and bar is a public event, design shops do a roaring trade, and avant-garde public spaces are more often than not publicly funded.

However, Barcelona is serious about work and money. Containing fifteen percent of Spain's population (1.7 million in the city itself), Catalonia produces more than twenty percent of the country's GDP and a third of all exports. This is a globalist city with a start-up culture rivalling that of London's or Berlin's. Many Big Tech companies are headquartered here, and the digital boom invites a new wave of expats and digital nomads settling in and around the city.

This is a sore point for locals, however, who resent the rising cost of rent, and the influx of people with only a fleeting connection to their city.

CATALAN INDEPENDENCE

Barcelona has long been considered different from the rest of Spain, and though visitors can attend a bullfight or flamenco show, this really isn't the place for such typically Spanish practices. The city is famous for its assured sense of independence and identity. Catalans have held onto their language tenaciously, defending it against repeated attempts from Castile, and the Franco government, to extinguish it. Above all, they believe Catalonia is a nation, not just a region.

While there are many who would prefer Barcelona to be the capital of an independent, Catalan-speaking nation, having gone so far as declaring independence in 2017 which resulted in the imposition of direct rule from Madrid, the majority of these hard-working people are simply frustrated that so much locally generated wealth is re-routed to Madrid.

All political considerations are cast aside, though, when seemingly the whole of Barcelona takes to the streets just before lunch or in the early evening. La Rambla, a tree-lined boulevard Victor Hugo dubbed the most beautiful in the world, is packed with locals and visitors. Boisterous patrons spill out of corner bars, mime artists strike poses for photos and spare change, and pavement restaurants hum with the chatter of its people-watching patrons.

Tapas is a fun communal dining experience

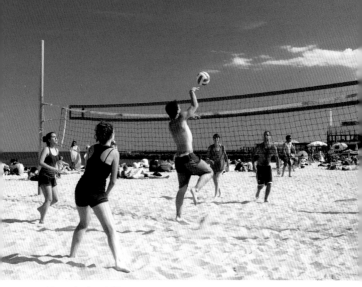

Easygoing beach life

EXPLORING ON FOOT

Barcelona is an ideal city for walking. Hemmed in by the sea, the River Besòs and hills on two sides, the city is surprisingly manageable on foot. It spills down a gentle slope to the beachfront. Near the water is the Barri Gòtic and the rest of the old city, a labyrinth of streets inhabited for a thousand years. Ancient stones of the Roman city can be seen in columns and walls, and it is possible to visit the settlement's original foundations beneath the Museu d'Història de la Ciutat.

Barcelona grew out of its original walls, and its modern districts extend in all directions. The avenues are broad and leafy, punctuated by squares crowded with cafés. The Eixample, a grid of streets laid out in the nineteenth century, is studded with landmark *modernista* apartment buildings, boutique stores, galleries, restaurants and hotels.

Barcelona is every bit as spirited at night as it is during the day. Residents begin their evenings with tapas and rounds of drinks after work, putting dinner off until late (10pm is normal). Live-music venues and clubs don't really get going until 2am. Any day of the week, La Rambla pulsates with life. If late-night Barcelona is too much for you, an evening stroll is rewarding: the cathedral, churches, palaces and monuments are beautiful illuminated at night. The Barri Gòtic retreats into silence, broken only by the animated hollering of late-night revellers or the rumble of skateboards.

SUSTAINABLE TRAVEL

Overtourism is a hot topic in Barcelona right now. Tourism has played a central role in Barcelona's spectacular growth since the 1992 Olympics. But, as visitor numbers continue to swell, a preponderance of short-term holiday rentals are pushing house prices up – and locals out. Barcelona's residential communities are worried. Famously, recent protests against overtourism culminated in tourists being sprayed with water. Don't let this stop you from enjoying the city: Catalans are friendly, welcoming folk. But it pays to be mindful of the cultural tensions at play. Consider booking a hotel or homestay instead of an Airbnb, perhaps in a lesser-visited but no-less enjoyable neighbourhood outside the centre (Barcelona has plenty). Choose family-run restaurants away from the main drags and avoid the souvenir kiosks along La Rambla (it's all made in China) and shop independent when you can.

Catalans are fatigued by the bar-crawling hedonism of tourists around the crowded Barceloneta beach. Avoid displays of over-exuberance, and don't walk around topless unless you're on the beach. Even better, you could travel or bike to one of Barcelona's several city beaches, such as Montgat, El Masnou and Premià de Mar, to avoid the crush (the city has a splendid infrastructure for cyclists; see page 127).

1

2

10 Things not to miss

3

4

5

6

A perfect day in Barcelona

9AM

La Rambla. Hit La Rambla early to enjoy the famous avenue before the crowds descend. Pick up your newspaper from a kiosk then pop into La Boqueria market for a proper Catalan breakfast like baby squid and poached eggs at *El Quim* (see page 118).

10.30AM

Barri Gòtic. East of La Rambla, the Barri Gòtic (Gothic Quarter) is a labyrinth of twisting streets and historic buildings. Meander through its shady, narrow lanes and palm-filled courtyards. Explore the heritage of the Old Town at the Museu d'Història de la Ciutat de Barcelona, or MUHBA (City History Museum; see page 43), before pausing for coffee in the diminutive *Mesón del Café* on Llibreteria (see page 117).

NOON

Basílica de Santa María del Mar. On the other side of Via Laietana is the El Born district. Glimpse the breathtaking interior of Santa María del Mar, or sip *una copa de cava* on the terrace of La Vinya del Senyor (see page 120) and admire the graceful church facade.

1.30PM

Lunchtime. Slip into the local rhythm with a wallet-friendly *menú del dia* in a neighbourhood bar like *Rodrigo* (see page 118) in Argenteria, or walk ten minutes to Barceloneta for paella by the sea at *Can Majó* (see page 123).

3.30PM

Siesta. Next, stroll along the Passeig Marítim towards the Vila Olímpica (see page 72), pausing for coffee in one of the waterfront *xiringuitos* (beach bars). Head back to base for a reviving siesta, essential if you are to keep up the pace until the small hours.

5.30PM

Explore the Eixample. Delve into the *modernista* streets of the Eixample, swinging by a Gaudí building, like La Pedrera or Casa Batlló, or just wander around the district to discover a wealth of extraordinary decorative details – from stained glass to ceramics – by his contemporaries (see page 57).

8.30PM

Drinks and tapas. Relax at one of the many terrace bars in elegant Rambla Catalunya, or try the eponymous cocktail at *Dry Martini* (see page 94) before feasting on tapas at *Tapas 24*, where chefs experiment with brave new takes on traditional recipes (see page 122).

10.30PM

On the town. Round off the day in style, just up the road at designer club *Mood Rooftop Bar* (Provença 277), part of *The One Barcelona*, an award-winning hotel where you can rub shoulders with the *beau monde*. Alternatively, catch a cab to *Mirablau*, a chic bar in Tibidabo with fine city views, and dance till dawn.

Offbeat Barcelona

8AM

Breakfast. Coffee can be a tad disappointing in Spain. Roasted with sugar, a process called *torrefacto*, it can taste a little burnt and sour, best served with lots of milk. However, coffee is treated as an artform at third-wave café *Maison Coffee*, which offers picturesque pistachio lattes and flaky pastries. Perfect for a light Mediterranean-style breakfast. See page 121.

9.30AM

Park Güell. Beat the crowds and afternoon heat and enjoy Gaudí's swirling candy-like masterpieces in Park Güell (see page 67). Don't miss the recently restored Casa-Museu Gaudí for some fresh insight (see page 69).

12.30PM

Market eats. Barcelona's main food market, La Boqueria is the place to go for lunch. Everything radiates out from the central fish and seafood kiosks – stalls piled with bunches of herbs, pots of spices, baskets of wild mushrooms, mounds of cheese and sausage, racks of bread and slabs of meat. And of course, there are excellent stand-up tapas bars for affordable eats. See page 35.

1PM

Whistlestop tour. Experience Barcelona from every angle on this unique three-hour tour (www.thetourguy.com). Start with a brief city walk to get your bearings in the Barri Gòtic and La Rambla. Afterwards, you'll fly high above

Barceloneta in a helicopter, with the beach and surrounding mountains unfurling beneath you. Bookings for the sailing trip are flexible, so you can save that for the following day if you've had your fill of adventure.

6PM

Treats made by nuns. In need of a pick-me-up? Hunker down for *frutas de almendra* (marzipan sweets) and coffee in the cosy basement crypt at *Caelum*, where the cakes and treats are baked in convents and monasteries across Spain. See page 116.

9PM

Rooftop light shows. Guarded by eerie sentinels and warriors, and framing the Sagrada Família, the hallucinatory rooftop terrace of Gaudí's Casa Milà is epic. At night, projection-mapping shows add an extra dimension of psychedelic otherworldliness. See page 60.

10PM

Traditional tapas. There's no sign above the wooden doors at *La Cova Fumada*, but it doesn't need to advertise. Claiming a tradition dating back to 1944, this old-school tavern attracts a loyal crowd – and it hasn't changed a bit. Rumours suggest this is the birthplace of *bombas* (mincemeat-filled breaded potato balls slathered in a spicy red sauce). The blackboard lays out the daily specials, with ingredients straight from the market. See page 123.

Barcelona on a budget

8AM

Breakfast. Pass up the overpriced hotel buffet and join the locals for breakfast in one of the city's bars, cafés or patisseries. A few euros will get you a hot drink and a brioche, croissant or sandwich just about anywhere. The traditional breakfast is *pa amb tomàquet* – bread rubbed with tomato, olive oil and garlic, perhaps topped with cured ham or sliced cheese.

9AM

The Catedral. Arrive in the morning, and you can wander around the ornate interior and lush cloister of the Catedral for free. Ride the lift up to the roof terrace and you're rewarded with intimate views of the cathedral towers and surrounding Gothic buildings and spires. It's by no means the highest vantage point in the city, but nowhere else do you feel so at the heart of medieval Barcelona. See page 40.

11AM

Bask on the beach. Unfurl a towel, slather on the sunblock and settle in for a relaxing day of golden sand and aquamarine waters at any of the city's eight beaches. Pack your own picnic or grab a *flauta* (filled baguette) en route to keep things cheap; beachside restaurants charge a premium for the prime location.

3PM

World-class art. Barcelona's city-run museums, including Museu Nacional d'Art de Catalunya (see page 79) and Museu Picasso (see page 54), offer free entry on certain afternoons and the first Sunday of the month. The schedule can feel a bit sporadic, so check the website to plan ahead.

4PM

Mercat de Sant Antoni. A living museum, Mercat de Sant Antoni (Carrer del Comte d'Urgell 1) is perpetually abuzz with the visceral sights and smells of caught-that-day fish, hanging hams and gleaming fruit and veg. This is a proper locals' market, and as you'd expect, it's where you'll find the freshest produce. Ideal for self-caterers, or for just stocking up on cheese, meat and olives. Cheap stand-up snacks are available at certain stalls and dotted around outside the market.

7PM

La Flor del Norte. A stumbling distance from the Barri Gòtic and La Barceloneta, *La Flor del Norte* does a thriving trade with locals, thanks to its exquisite seafood at pinch-me prices. A sizzling hot, saffron-coloured paella arrives in a giant terracotta pot (easily enough for two) for €14. See page 123.

9PM

Bodega Cal Marino. At this stone-walled tavern, the wines in the barrels are to take away at knockdown prices, and you can drink a copa for €2. There's also a more sophisticated selection on offer in the cavernous bar. See page 94.

History

Barcelona was originally called Barcino, named after the Carthaginian general and father of Hannibal, Hamilcar Barca, who established a base on the northeastern coast of Iberia in the third century BC. Phoenicians and Greeks had previously settled the area, but the Romans, who conquered all of Iberia, left the most indelible marks on Barcelona. They defeated the Carthaginians at Ilipa in 206 BC and ruled Spain for the next six hundred years, a period in which Roman law, language and culture took root across the peninsula. The Roman citadel in Barcelona, surrounded by a massive wall, occupied high ground where the cathedral, Catalan government building and city hall now stand. From the first century AD, Christian communities spread throughout Catalonia.

King Ferdinand and Queen Isabella greet Columbus

MERCANTILE NATION

Successive generations turned their attention towards the conquest of the Mediterranean basin. Its mercantilist trade grew rapidly, and its territories included Sardinia, Corsica, Naples and Roussillon in southern France. The Middle Ages, from the late thirteenth to the fifteenth century, was a time of significant building in Barcelona, giving rise to the cathedral and other great Gothic palaces and monuments. Barcelona also served as a channel for the exchange of scientific knowledge and scholarship between the Arab world and the West. The arts and culture flourished, patronised by

NOTES

While much of Spain was under Moorish domination, Catalonia remained linked to Europe. This has done much to determine the distinctive Catalan character.

a vigorous class of artisans, bankers and merchants, including an important Jewish community.

WAR AND RESISTANCE

In 1640, with Spain and France involved in the Thirty Years' War, Catalonia declared itself an independent republic, allied to France. Spanish troops besieged and captured Barcelona in 1651 and, after the French defeat in 1659, Catalan territories north of the Pyrenees were ceded to France, fixing the border where it is today. The ensuing years were rife with wars and disputes over succession to the crown, in which Barcelona automatically sided with whichever faction opposed Madrid.

The worst of these episodes came in the War of the Spanish Succession (1701–14) between the backers of Philip of Anjou, grandson of Louis XIV of France, and the Habsburg claimant, Archduke Charles of Austria. Charles was enthusiastically received when he landed in Catalonia, but Philip, supported by France, won the war and became the first Bourbon ruler, Philip V. After a thirteen-month siege, on 11 September 1714, the royal army captured and sacked Barcelona. The Catalan Generalitat was dissolved, and the city's privileges abolished. The Ciutadella fortress was built to keep the populace subdued, and official use of the Catalan language was outlawed. Catalonia celebrates this date as its national holiday, the Diada, a symbol of the spirit of nationalist resistance.

Showcasing the maritime empire's glory in the Museu Marítim

The spirit of European liberalism was late in reaching Spain. After many reverses, a republic, a constitutional monarchy and a democratic constitution were instituted in 1873. Shortly afterwards, Barcelona was at long last given the right to trade with the colonies of the New World.

INDUSTRIALISATION

Meanwhile, the city had continued about its business, devoting its energies to industrialisation. Barcelona's medieval walls were torn down to make way for expansion in the mid-nineteenth century. The Eixample district was laid out on a grid of broad avenues where the new industrialists built mansions. Wealthy patrons supported architects such as Antoni Gaudí and Lluís Domènech i Montaner. Prosperity was accompanied by a revival in arts and letters, a period known in Catalan as the Renaixença (Renaissance). The city bid for worldwide recognition with the Universal Exposition of 1888, on the site of the Ciutadella fortress, today's Parc de la Ciutadella.

With the industrial expansion, an urban working class evolved. Agitation for social justice and regional ferment created a combustible atmosphere, and the city became the scene of strikes and violence. In 1914 a provincial government, the Mancomunitat, was formed, uniting the four Catalan provinces – Barcelona, Tarragona, Lleida and Girona. It was dissolved in 1923 by General Primo de Rivera, who established a military dictatorship and banned the Catalan language.

CIVIL WAR

In 1931, the Second Republic was established, and King Alfonso XIII escaped to exile. Catalonia won a charter establishing home rule, restoration of the regional parliament and flag, and recognition of Catalan as the official language. Elements in the Spanish army rebelled in 1936, initiating the brutal Civil War. Many churches in Barcelona were put to the torch by anti-clerical mobs. Barcelona was one of the last cities to fall to the rebel troops of General Francisco Franco at the war's end in 1939.

The Civil War culminated with some 700,000 combatants dead; another 30,000 were executed, including many priests and nuns; perhaps as many as 15,000 civilians were killed in air raids, and numerous refugees fled the country. Catalonia paid a heavy price in defeat. Franco abolished all regional

> **NOTES**
>
> Despite the Primo de Rivera dictatorship (1923–30), Barcelona plunged into preparations for the 1929 International Exhibition, with the creation of monumental buildings and sports facilities on the hill of Montjuïc, many of which can still be seen today. It opened just before the Wall Street Crash.

Aerial view of the city after bombing by the Italian Air Force, 1938

institutions and established central controls. The Catalan language was proscribed, even in schools and churches. For years, Barcelona received little financial support from Madrid, and Spain remained essentially cut off from the rest of Europe.

1960 ONWARDS

Despite this cultural and political repression, by the 1960s the industrious Catalans were forging ahead, making this corner of Spain the most economically successful in the country. The traditional textile sector was overtaken by the more prosperous iron, steel and chemical industries, which called for manpower, so people from the less prosperous rural regions of Spain flocked to Barcelona. Sprawling suburbs with ugly high-rise buildings mushroomed around the city. Franco's government also promoted tourism in the 1960s, and crowds began to descend on the Costa Brava. Speculators exploited the coastline, and the economy boomed.

The dictatorship ended with Franco's death in 1975. Juan Carlos, grandson of Alfonso XIII, became king and Spain made a rapid and successful transition to democracy. In Barcelona, cava flowed in the streets on the day Franco died and the Generalitat was restored as the governing body of the autonomous region. The Catalan language was made official, and a renaissance of culture and traditions followed, seen in literature, theatre, television, films, cultural centres, arts festivals and popular fiestas.

In Barcelona the charismatic Socialist mayor, Pasqual Maragall, shaped today's modern city by using the 1992 Olympics as an excuse to start a radical programme of urban reform to remedy years of neglect by central government. The momentum of this drive continued after the Olympics and launched Barcelona into the twenty-first century, under Mayor Jordi Hereu. Urban, economic and social refurbishment has been implemented, clearing old industrial areas such as Poble Nou, improving transport links and making way for high-tech industries and new business hotels. Despite hard economic times, which have slowed the building process, Barcelona enjoys a high-profile status as a top business and conference centre and ranks high among European cities for its quality of life.

Recent years have been marked by ongoing development and modernisation of the city as well as rising tensions between the Catalan authorities, led by nationalist Artur Mas and his successor Carles Puigdemont, and Madrid. Successive Catalan cabinets have been pushing strongly for secession from Spain with the Catalan assembly passing a controversial eighteen-month 'roadmap' to independence at the beginning of 2016. In 2017 and 2018, this unfolded in full-blown crisis as the Catalonian leaders backed an independence referendum which was declared illegal by the government in Madrid. Eventually, direct rule was imposed, Puigdemont fled the country, and Spain issued a European arrest warrant for his return.

Barcelona fell to the rebel troops of General Francisco Franco at the end of the Civil War in 1939

Many Catalan leaders were arrested, and some charged with rebellion. The issue of independence will not dissipate any time soon.

CHRONOLOGY

237 BC Carthaginian Hamilcar Barca makes his base at Barcino.

206 BC Romans defeat Carthaginians in Battle of Ilipa.

AD 531–54 Barcelona becomes the capital of the Visigoths.

711 Moorish invasion of Spain. They remain there till 1492.

878 Wilfred 'the Hairy', Count of Barcelona, creates hereditary passage of titles.

1096–1131 Ramón Berenguer III extends Catalan empire.

1359 Corts Catalanes (Parliament of Catalonia) established.

1469 Ferdinand and Isabella unite Aragón and Castile.

1494 Administration of Catalonia put under Castilian control.

1659 Catalan territories north of Pyrenees ceded to France.

1701–14 War of Spanish Succession.

1713–14 Siege of Barcelona by Felipe V's forces; Ciutadella built.

1808–14 Peninsular War between England and France.

1888 Barcelona hosts its first Universal Exposition.

1914 Mancomunitat (provincial government) formed in Catalonia.

1923 General Primo de Rivera sets up dictatorship and bans Catalan language.

1932 Catalonia granted short-lived statute of independence.

1936–9 Civil War ends in Franco's rule and isolation of Spain.

1975 Franco dies; Juan Carlos becomes king.

1979 Statute of Autonomy; Catalan restored as official language.

1986 Spain joins European Community (European Union).

1992 Barcelona hosts the Olympics.

2006 A new statute is passed, giving Catalonia more autonomy.

2009 High-tech business district 22@ forges ahead successfully.

2011 Xavier Trias of the Catalan Nationalist party is elected mayor.

2014 80 percent of voters say 'yes' to Catalonia's separation from Spain in a non-binding referendum.

2015 Regional and municipal elections shake-up the Catalonian political scene. Ada Colau, a social activist, becomes mayor.

2016 Despite strong opposition from the Spanish government, Carles Puigdemont embarks on an 18-month campaign for independence.

2017 On 17 August 2017, 13 people are killed and 130 are injured when a van is deliberately driven into pedestrians on La Rambla.

2018 Spain withdraws its European Arrest Warrant for Carles Puigdemont after a German court rules that he cannot be extradited for rebellion.

2020 Spanish Grand Prix, one of the world's oldest competitive Formula One races, is to be held at the Circuit de Barcelona-Catalunya.

2026 Expected completion date of Sagrada Família, 100 years after Gaudi's death.

Gaudí's whimsical Palau Güell

Places

Barcelona can be approached by neighbourhood or by theme. You can set out to explore the Barri Gòtic (Gothic Quarter), Montjuïc hill or the waterfront, or you can create a tour around the works of Gaudí and *modernisme* or the latest cutting-edge architecture. It's very tempting to try to sandwich everything into your stay, but leave time to be side-tracked by a colourful food market, to duck down a hidden alley of antiques shops or to peek into a quiet courtyard. There's no better way to pass a couple of hours than to sit at a pavement café while you linger over a drink, read a book and simply watch the world go by.

In the Old Town – Barri Gòtic, La Ribera, El Raval, La Rambla – and the Eixample district, the best way to travel is on foot. For sights further afield, including Montjuïc, Barceloneta and the waterfront, Tibidabo, La Sagrada Família and Park Güell, it's best to make use of Barcelona's excellent public transport network – clean and efficient metro, suburban trains, modern buses, funiculars, trams and cable cars (see page 139).

LA RAMBLA

HIGHLIGHTS

» Canaletes, see page 32
» Rambla de les Flors, see page 33
» La Boqueria, see page 35
» Palau Güell, see page 37
» Plaça Reial, see page 37

To call **La Rambla ❶** a street is to do it woeful injustice. Perhaps Europe's most famous boulevard – energetic, artistic, democratic and a touch decadent – it is an intoxicating parade of humanity. It's at its best in the morning or in the early evening, while in the small hours it's populated by a motley mix of newspaper-sellers, street-sweepers and late-night revellers stumbling back to their apartments and hotels.

The broad, tree-shaded promenade stretches nearly 1.5km (one mile) down a gentle incline from the city's hub, Plaça de Catalunya (see page 63), to the waterfront. La Rambla takes its name from an Arabic word meaning a sandy, dry riverbed; it was a shallow gully until the fourteenth century, when Barcelona families began to build homes nearby. As the area became more populated, the stream was soon paved over. To the north of La Rambla (left as you walk down it) is the Barri Gòtic; to the south, or right, is El Raval.

CANALETES

The five sections of La Rambla change in character, as they do in name (hence it is often called 'Les Rambles'), as you stroll along. The short **Rambla de Canaletes** at the top, named after the **Font de Canaletes**, the fountain that is one of the symbols of the city,

---

WHERE TO SHOOT THE BEST PICTURES

Barcelona is brazenly beautiful, and photo opportunities abound. Park Güell's opulent display of swirling Gaudí masterpieces is a good place to start (see page 67). From the mosaiced, meandering walls of the park's viewpoint, there's an unbeatable shot of Gaudí's Barcelona in the foreground, the sprawling city and the Med visible in the distance. Arrive early to capture the soft light of the morning sun fall on La Sagrada Família and its celestial-looking basilica (see page 65). Barri Gòtic's lattice of narrow, meandering streets is seriously photogenic – especially around Carrer del Bisbe (see page 67). For a fully panoramic view of the city, trundle up to the bunkers of Carmel, a hillside vantage point where you spot the cast of Barcelona's star landmarks, against a backdrop of mountain and sea.

The vibrant atmosphere of La Rambla is palpable

is where crowds pour in from the Plaça de Catalunya or spill out from the metro and railway stations beneath. On Sunday and Monday in football season you'll find noisy knots of fans verbally replaying the games of Barça, Barcelona's beloved football club; if an important match has just been won, watch out for the fireworks.

FLOWERS AND PASTRIES

Next is **Rambla dels Estudis**, popularly called **Rambla dels Ocells** (Rambla of the Birds) as it was a traditional bird market, and **Rambla de les Flors**, officially the **Rambla de Sant Josep**. People flock here on 23 April, the feast day of Sant Jordi (St George), patron saint of Catalonia, celebrated as Day of the Book because it is also the anniversary of Cervantes' and Shakespeare's deaths in 1616.

La Boqueria market

A woman traditionally gives her man a book, and a man gives his woman a rose – both of which are available in abundance along La Rambla. Keep your eyes peeled on the right side of the road for the delectable *modernista* pastry and chocolate shop, **Escribà** (Antiga Casa Figueres; www.escriba.es), its fanciful swirls on the outside a match for the delicacies within. An ideal spot to pause for coffee.

Facing La Rambla is the elegant **Palau de la Virreina** (La Rambla 99; http://ajuntament.barcelona.cat/lavirreina/ca; free), a grand palace completed in 1778 for the young widow of the viceroy of colonial Peru. The palace is partially open for cultural events and major exhibitions, and houses a branch of the city's Department of Culture where you can find out what is currently on in the city and buy tickets for performances and shows.

LA BOQUERIA

On the right-hand side of the street is one of La Rambla's great attractions: the **Mercat de Sant Josep**, usually called **La Boqueria** ❷ (www.boqueria.barcelona). This ornate, nineteenth-century covered market is a cornucopia of delights for the senses: fresh fish, meats, sausages, fruits and vegetables, all kinds of spices, neatly braided ropes of garlic, sun-dried tomatoes and peppers, preserves and sweetmeats. The market is also a vibrant community, where shoppers and merchants greet each other by name, ribald sallies across the aisles set off gales of laughter, and the freshness of the *rape* (an angler fish popular in Catalonia) is debated with passion.

La Boqueria is laid out beneath high-ceilinged ironwork naves, like a railway station, with restaurants scattered in and near the market. The best time to visit is when practised shoppers and restaurateurs go – early in the morning.

The heart of La Rambla is nearby, at the Pla de la Boqueria, a busy intersection near the Liceu metro station paved with an unmistakable Joan Miró mosaic. Here stands one of Europe's great opera houses, the **Gran Teatre del Liceu** (www.liceubarcelona. cat), inaugurated in 1861.

Palau de la Virreina, home to the city's Department of Culture

Montserrat Caballé and Josep Carreras made their reputations singing at this theatre, a monument of the Catalan Renaissance and favourite haunt of the elite set. The opera house was gutted by a fire in 1994 then stunningly restored and extended, and eventually reopened in 1999.

Directly across La Rambla is the *Cafè de l'Òpera* (www.cafeoperabcn.com), a handsome, *modernista*-style haunt that's always busy and retains a local feel despite being popular with tourists. It's a good spot for refreshment before you push on down the **Rambla**

The opulent interiors of Gaudí-designed Palau Güell, created for textile tycoon Count Eusebi Güell

dels Caputxins. La Rambla's character, like the incline, plummets downhill after the Liceu, but the street-entertainment factor rises in inverse proportion. Wade your way through jugglers, human statues, fire-eaters, tarot-card readers, lottery-ticket sellers, hair-braiders and street artists rapidly knocking out portraits, caricatures and chalk masterworks on the pavement.

PALAU GÜELL

On the right side of the street is the **Hotel Oriente**, which preserves a seventeenth-century Franciscan convent and cloister inside. Note the naïve painted angels floating over the doorway of what was Ernest Hemingway's favourite Barcelona lodging. Just beyond, on

Carrer Nou de la Rambla is **Palau Güell ❸** (www.palauguell.cat), the mansion that Gaudí (see page 64) masterminded in 1885 for his principal patron, textile tycoon Count Eusebi Güell. This extraordinary building is arranged around an enormous salon, from which a conical mosaic-tiled roof emerges to preside over an unusual landscape of capriciously placed battlements, balustrades and curiously shaped chimneys.

PLAÇA REIAL
Returning to La Rambla, cross over into the arcaded **Plaça Reial**. This handsome, spacious square is graced with a fountain, palm trees, and wrought-iron lampposts designed by the young Gaudí.

The curious chimneys and battlements crowning Palau
Güell could only be the brainchild of Gaudí

Like La Boqueria market and other landmarks, this *plaça* came into being as a result of the destruction of a convent, when church property was expropriated in the mid-nineteenth century. Today, this fun and lively place is lined with bars, cafés and restaurants whose tables spill out onto the pavement, and buzzes with action night and day.

Leading down to the harbour is the short **Rambla de Santa Mònica**, beginning at the Plaça del Teatre, site of the Teatre Principal. The warren of alleys to the right, once known as the **Barri Xino**, while cleaned up a bit, is still pretty seedy and not the best place for a midnight stroll, but some of the old bars are becoming fashionable again. If you're after a taste of yesteryear Barcelona, the tiny, atmospheric *Pastís* bar (Carrer Santa Mònica 4, www.bar-pastis.com) hasn't changed since opening in 1947.

Carrer dels Escudellers, a busy pedestrian street on the other side of La Rambla, is the gateway to an enclave of clubs, bars, restaurants and trendy boutiques, and the delights of the Barri Gòtic. At its far end, Plaça George Orwell has become a trendy place to congregate.

Back on La Rambla, **Centre d'Art Santa Mònica** (http://artssanta monica.gencat.cat) is an avant-garde contemporary arts centre in a seventeenth-century convent. Nearer the port is the **Museu de Cera ❹** (www.museocerabcn.com), a tourist trap with over three hundred wax effigies. La Rambla ends at the broad, open space facing the **Mirador de Colom**, a statue honouring Christopher Columbus, where a lift ascends to the top for good views of the port. Just beyond lies Barcelona's revitalised waterfront.

BARRI GÒTIC

HIGHLIGHTS

From its beginnings more than two thousand years ago, Barcelona has grown outwards in concentric rings, like ripples on a pond. The ancient core is a hill the Romans called Mont Tàber, where they raised a temple to Augustus Caesar and in the fourth century AD built high walls about 1.5km (one mile) long to protect their settlement. This is the nucleus of the medieval district called the **Barri Gòtic** or Gothic Quarter, with its remarkable concentration

Palm-lined Plaça Reial

The Catedral facade

of medieval palaces and churches, many built on Roman foundations.

THE CATEDRAL

The best place to begin a tour is the superb **Catedral** ❺ (www.catedralbcn.org; free during worship hours, charge for seeing the choir and the roof), the neighbourhood's focal point. It was begun in 1298 on the site of earlier churches going back to the times of the Visigoths. The final touch – the florid Gothic facade – was not completed until the end of the nineteenth century and thus contrasts with the simple, octagonal towers. The ribs of the cathedral's high vault are joined at carved and painted keystone medallions, a typically Catalan feature. In the centre of the nave is a splendid Gothic choir with lacy spires.

Steps beneath the altar lead to the alabaster tomb of Santa Eulàlia, one of the city's two patron saints, martyred in the fourth century and celebrated with a *Festa Major* in February. On the wall of the right aisle are the tombs of Count Ramón Berenguer I and his wife Almodis, who founded an earlier cathedral on this spot in 1058. The Catalan Gothic altarpieces of the Transfiguration painted for the Sant Salvador chapel in the fifteenth century by Bernat Martorell are considered his masterpiece.

The leafy cloister, which now also contains a gift shop, is a lively refuge, with birds fluttering among the orange, magnolia and palm trees and inhabited by thirteen geese, symbolising the age of Eulàlia when she died. Watch where you walk, as the cloister is paved with tombstones, badly worn, but many still bearing the ancient emblems of the bootmakers', tailors' and other craft guilds whose wealth helped pay for the cathedral. From the cloister, pass to the **Capella de Santa Llúcia**, a chapel with thirteenth- and fourteenth-century tombstones on the floor and a monument to an armoured crusader knight on one wall.

Leaving the chapel by its front entrance, turn left into Carrer del Bisbe. Look up as you walk through the Old Town to take in the details – a curious hanging sign, a lantern, an unusual sculpture or plants trailing from balconies. On the right is a row of gargoyles leaning from the roof of the Palau de la Generalitat, where there

Barri Gòtic's grand Catedral

is also a richly ornamented gateway. The lacy overhead bridge is Gothic in style but is actually a 1929 addition.

PLAÇA SANT JAUME

Just ahead is the **Plaça Sant Jaume ❻**, the heart of the Barri Gòtic, where the Government of Catalonia, the Generalitat, faces the Casa de la Ciutat (city hall, also known as the Ajuntament; guided tours English; free). Though the institutions they house are not always in agreement, the two buildings are a harmonious pair: both have classical facades that hide their Gothic origins.

The **Palau de la Generalitat**, on the north side of the square, is the more interesting of the two. It dates from 1359, when it was made the executive branch, reporting to the Corts Catalanes (referred to as the 'first parliament in Europe').

Palau de la Generalitat

The nucleus of the present building is the main patio – pure Catalan Gothic, with an open staircase leading to a gallery of arches on slender pillars. The star feature here is the flamboyant Gothic facade of the **Capella de Sant Jordi**. The **Saló de Sant Jordi**, a vaulted hall in the seventeenth-century front block of the building, is lined with modern murals of historical scenes. It is open to the only on a few days each year. It is best to check the dates and times and book your ticket in advance at www.president.cat.

The **Ajuntament** across the plaza, has held Barcelona's city hall since 1372. It was here that the Consell de Cent, a council of one hundred notable citizens, met to deal with civic affairs under the watchful eyes of the king. The original entrance can be seen around the left corner of the building, on the Carrer de la Ciutat. Inside, the left staircase leads to the upper gallery of the old courtyard and to the **Saló de Cent** (Hall of the One Hundred) with a barrel-vaulted ceiling. The red-and-yellow bars of Catalonia's flag decorate the walls. The hall where the city council now meets adjoins, and at the head of the black marble staircase is the **Saló de les Cròniques** (Hall of the Chronicles), noted for the modern murals in sepia tones by Josep Maria Sert. From behind the Ajuntament, take Carrer d'Hèrcules to Plaça Sant Just for a peek at the church of **Sants Just i Pastor** and the pretty little square on which it sits, evocative of a bygone Barcelona. The church is one of the oldest in the city, though it was repeatedly remodelled. It is said that any will sworn before its altar is recognised as valid by the courts of Barcelona, a practice dating from the tenth century.

> **NOTES**
>
> The Plaça Sant Jaume is the meeting place for the giants (*gegants*), the huge regal figures that process through the streets at the festival of La Mercè, one of Barcelona's patron saints (with Santa Eulàlia), in September. It is also where you will see *castells* – human towers reaching nine people high – an attraction at various fiestas.

PLAÇA DEL REI

From Plaça Sant Just, take Dagueria, cross over Jaume I and follow the street up to Baixada Llibreteria, home to one of Barcelona's oldest and tiniest coffee shops, *El Mesón del Café*. One block down on the left is Veguer, which leads to the **Plaça del Rei** and the **Museu d'Història de la Ciutat de Barcelona** ❼ (MUHBA; City History Museum; www.barcelona.cat/museuhistoria/ca). The building is a Gothic mansion that was moved stone by stone to this location. In the basement, excavations have uncovered a portion of the Roman city, including shops running along the inside of the Roman wall. Dyeing vats for a clothing industry and evidence of winemaking have been unearthed. Most importantly, however, evidence has been revealed of an early church on the site with a bishop's residence, which provides the link between the Roman and medieval cities. A lift takes visitors down to view the subterranean city. Above them is the **Palau Reial Major** (Royal Palace), which acted as the residence for the Kings of Aragón, and into which you emerge at the end of the excavations. The main buildings here are the chapel, tower and great hall. The **Capella de Santa Àgata** (Chapel of St Agatha) is notable for the fifteenth-century altarpiece

Plaça del Rei

of the *Adoration of the Magi* by one of Catalonia's finest artists, Jaume Huguet.

The vast, barrel-vaulted great hall or throne room, the **Saló del Tinell**, was built for royal audiences in 1359 under Pere III (the Ceremonius) by Guillem Carbonell. On occasion the Corts Catalanes (Parliament) met here. This is where Ferdinand and Isabella supposedly received Columbus in 1493 on his return from his first voyage to the Americas. It was later used as a church, and by the Inquisition, whose victims were burned at the stake in the square.

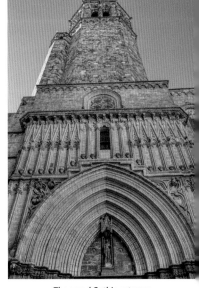

The grand Gothic entrance of Palau Reial Major

Concerts are held in the square in summer.

Behind the Royal Palace, off Carrer Tapineria, is Plaça de Berenguer el Gran, which has a well-preserved section of the original Roman wall. The defences were nine metres (30ft) high, 3.5 metres (12ft) thick and marked at intervals by towers eighteen metres (59ft) tall. Until 1943, most of this section was covered by old houses, which were removed to restore the walls to view.

TOWARDS THE MUSEU FREDERIC MARÈS

A former wing of the palace that encloses the Plaça del Rei was rebuilt in 1557 to become the **Palau del Lloctinent** (Palace of the Lieutenant), residence of the king's representative. It has been beautifully renovated and can now be visited, via an entrance on

A shady courtyard at the Museu Frederic Marès

Carrer dels Comtes. Notice its elegant patio with a noble staircase and remarkable carved wooden ceiling. Just beyond, flanking the cathedral, is the **Museu Frederic Marès ❽** (www.museumares.bcn. cat), which has a beautiful courtyard with an attractive summer café. Marès, a twentieth-century sculptor of civic statues, was a compulsive collector who bequeathed to Barcelona an idiosyncratic curation of art dating from the ancient world up through the nineteenth century. The lower floors house sculpture. The collector's cabinet takes up the second and third floors, described as 'a museum within a museum'.

ROMAN REMAINS AND THE JEWISH GHETTO

Retracing your steps on the narrow street flanking the cathedral, circle around to the rear and duck into the narrow Carrer del Paradís. Here, just inside the doorway of the Centre Excursionista de Catalunya, four columns of the Roman Temple of Augustus are embedded in the wall. This slender lane takes you back into Plaça Sant Jaume. Streets radiate in all directions, each an invitation to explore the Barri Gòtic. The **Carrer del Call** leads into the maze of crooked streets that was the Call, or Jewish Quarter, until the late fourteenth century. Today the quarter bustles with antiques shops and dealers of rare books, plus bars and restaurants frequented by antiquarians and artists. Just off St Domènec del Call is the **Centre d'Interpretació del Call** (Placeta de Mannel Ribé), a branch of the history museum and an information centre on this historic area.

Meander into Baixada de Santa Eulàlia. Just off it is the tiny **Plaça Sant Felip Neri**, a peaceful square, where the church was pockmarked by Italian bombs during the Civil War. Boutique hotel *Neri*, set in two historical houses with one being a twelfth-century medieval palace, has a privileged view of the scene.

ANTIQUE ALLEY

The Baixada de Santa Eulàlia descends to **Carrer de Banys Nous**, named for the long-gone twelfth-century 'new' baths of the ghetto. This winding street, which follows the line of the old Roman wall,

---

EL CALL

Barcelona's Jews, though noted as doctors, scholars and jewellers, were confined to El Call and forced to wear long, hooded cloaks with yellow headbands. Taxation of the community was a source of royal income. This did not save El Call from being burned and looted as persecution of the Jews throughout Spain mounted in the thirteenth and fourteenth centuries. Eventually, the Jews of Barcelona were killed, expelled or forcibly converted to Christianity, and their synagogues were turned into churches. Just off Carrer del Call, at Carrer de Marlet 1, a medieval inscription in Hebrew marks the site of a hospital founded by one 'Rabbi Samuel Hassareri, may his life never cease'.

Inside Santa Maria del Pi

is the unofficial boundary of the Barri Gòtic. It is also known as the Carrer dels Antiquaris – the street of antique dealers. Keep your eyes peeled for unusual hand-painted shop signs, the fretwork of Gothic balconies, and dusty treasures in the shop windows. You will also notice the time-worn tile signs with a cart symbol high on the walls, the indication of one-way streets.

A TRIO OF PLAZAS

Around the corner is a trio of impossibly pretty plazas. **Plaça Sant Josep Oriol** adjoins **Plaça del Pi**, on which sits **Santa Maria del Pi ❾**, a handsome Catalan Gothic church with a tall, octagonal bell tower and a harmonious facade pierced by a large fifteenth-century rose window. 'Pi' means pine tree, and there is a small one here replacing the landmark specimen of past centuries. Buildings in the plaza show the *sgrafitto* technique of scraping designs in coloured plaster, imported from Italy in the early 1700s. Barcelona's emerging merchant class favoured such facades as an inexpensive substitute for the sculptures on aristocratic palaces.

These adjoining squares, together with the smaller **Placeta del Pi** to the rear of the church, are the essence of old Barcelona and a great place to while away the hours. The bars with tables spread out beneath leafy trees are magnets for young people and visitors, who are entertained by roving musicians. On Saturdays and Sundays, artists typically offer their canvases for sale in lively Plaça Sant Josep Oriol, where the *Bar del Pi* is a popular meeting place. At weekends, a farmers' market selling cheeses, bread and honey is set up in the Plaça del Pi. From here, the street that leads north – **Carrer Petritxol** – is one of the Barri Gòtic's most traditional. The narrow alley is lined with art galleries, framing shops and traditional *granjas* – good stops for pastries and hot chocolate. Barcelona's oldest (open since 1877) and most famous art gallery is **Sala Parés** (http://salapares.com) at No. 5.

Carrer Petritxol, one of the Barri Gòtic's most atmospheric streets

AROUND PLAÇA NOVA

At Carrer Portaferrisa, a left turn will take you to La Rambla, while a right turn will loop back to the cathedral and a handful

El Corte Inglés department store on Plaça de Catalunya

of additional sights on the perimeter of the Barri Gòtic. (You could also return to Plaça Sant Josep Oriol and follow Carrer de la Palla.) In **Plaça Nova**, in front of the cathedral, is the Col.legi d'Arquitectes (Architects' Association). Picasso designed the graffiti-like drawings of the Three Kings and children bearing palm branches that are etched on the 1960s facade. For three weeks in December, a market selling Nativity figures and Christmas trees occupies the Plaça Nova – a square that got its name, 'New', in 1356 and has held markets for nearly a thousand years. Look for the strange, quintessential Catalan figure, *el caganer* – the red-capped peasant squatting and defecating beside the manger.

The pedestrian thoroughfare that pushes north to Plaça de Catalunya is **Avinguda Portal de l'Àngel**, one of the city's main shopping streets, where you will find the usual international brands such as Zara and Pull&Bear. It is especially busy when *rebaixes* (sales) are on. Look for little Carrer Montsió, which leads to **Els Quatre Gats** (The Four Cats; see page 118), a bar and restaurant that became famous when Picasso and a group of young intellectuals – painters Ramón Casas and Santiago Rusiñol among them – frequented it. Picasso had his first exhibition here in 1901, and the bar, one of the first commissions for the *modernista* architect Puig i Cadafalch, preserves its turn-of-the-twentieth-century ambience and is, understandably, a great favourite with visitors to Barcelona.

LA RIBERA

HIGHLIGHTS

Some of the most beautiful Gothic architecture and most fascinating medieval corners of Barcelona lie just outside the Barri Gòtic on the

Passeig del Born, a pretty plaza in El Born

other side of Via Laietana – a traffic-filled avenue roughly parallel to the Ramblas, which was cut through the city in 1859 to link the port with the modern centre (the Eixample). This atmospheric quarter, **La Ribera**, is home to the Museu Picasso and the majestic church of **Santa Maria del Mar** ❿ (www.santamariadelmarbarcelona.org). Carrer de l'Argenteria cuts a diagonal swathe from Plaça de l'Angel to the church. Begun in 1329 at the height of Catalonia's expansion as a Mediterranean power, it is the greatest example of pure Catalan Gothic, with unadorned exterior walls, a sober facade flanked by three-tiered octagonal bell towers, and a beautiful rose window over the portal.

The dimensions and austerity of the interior are breathtaking. Fires during Civil War rioting in 1936 consumed all the trappings of

The Catalan Gothic architecture of Santa Maria del Mar

chapels, choir and altar, leaving the interior stripped to its essence. The result is a lofty hall suffused with soft light from the stained-glass windows. Three naves are supported by slim, octagonal columns set thirteen metres (43ft) apart, and the dimensions of the interior are multiples of this distance, achieving a perfect symmetry. Behind the simple altar, the columns branch high overhead into the arched vaulting of the apse. Keep an eye out for the colourful restored keystones starting at the entrance.

The acoustics are excellent, best demonstrated by the concerts held in the church.

EL BORN

The rear door of the church leads to the **Passeig del Born**, a pretty, rectangular plaza where jousts were held in the Middle Ages and which today is the nucleus of this fashionable enclave, full of smart galleries, restaurants, bars and chic shops. Many of the little streets surrounding the church are named after the guilds of the craftspeople who once worked here, such as *sombrerers* (hatmakers), *mirallers* (mirror-makers) and *espasería* (sword-makers). The area is better known now for the people who fill its designer bars late into the night and spill out onto the streets. At the end, the magnificent, wrought-iron **El Born Centre Cultural**, or Born CMM (http://elborn culturaimemoria.barcelona.cat), the old fruit-and-vegetable market, has been converted into a museum and cultural centre hostings concerts and exhibitions. It features the archaeological ruins of a medieval city and shows how life was here from 1713 to 1714.

CARRER MONTCADA AND THE MUSEU PICASSO

One of Barcelona's grandest medieval streets, **Carrer Montcada**, populated by aristocrats from the fourteenth to the sixteenth centuries, is lined with splendid Gothic palaces, each with an imposing door or arched gate to an inner courtyard from where an ornamental staircase usually led up to reception rooms. These grand abodes were gradually abandoned after the demolition of the adjoining district and construction of the Ciutadella fortress. This quarter is the most authentically medieval part of the city. At No. 25, **Moco Museum** (www.mocomuseum.com) offers a permanent collection of big-hitters from the Pop Art world (Keith Haring and Banksy feature), plus more leftfield exhibitions, in its calming white-walled gallery, formerly a sixteenth-century palace.

Further along, at No. 12, the **Museo Etnológico y de Culturas del Mundo** (http://museuculturesmon.bcn.cat) highlights the Native arts of South America and the non-Western world, incorporating the collection of the now-closed Museu Etnològic.

Across the street, the **Museu Picasso** ⓫ (www.museupicasso. bcn.es) is spread across a string of five palaces. The main entrance is through the fifteenth-century **Palau Aguilar**. The buildings were acquired by the city to house the collection of paintings, drawings and ceramics donated by Picasso's lifelong friend and secretary, Jaume Sabartés. After the museum opened in 1963, Picasso added sketches and paintings from his childhood and youth. As a teenager he produced large canvases in the nineteenth-century realist style,

---

PABLO PICASSO

The world's most acclaimed twentieth-century artist, Pablo Ruiz y Picasso was born in 1881 in Málaga, the son of an art teacher, whose work took the family to Barcelona. Picasso began his art studies here and became part of a group of innovative artists and writers. In 1900, Picasso first visited Paris, and settled there four years later. He never returned to Barcelona after 1934. Even had he wanted to do so, his opposition to the Franco regime would have made it impossible, but his work always retained strong Spanish links. When Picasso died in 1973 (two years before the death of Franco and the end of the dictatorship), the bulk of his own collection, now in the Musée Picasso in Paris, went to the French government in a deal to settle taxes.

Museu Picasso

such as the *First Communion* and *Science and Charity*. The collection of his work is the largest outside Paris, and while it doesn't possess any of his finest pieces, it does have two good examples of his Blue Period (1901–4), as well as *The Harlequin* (1917), and the idiosyncratic *Las Meninas* series, the variations on the theme of the Velázquez masterpiece in Madrid's Prado Museum, which provides a fascinating view of Picasso's innovative approach to his subject.

Opposite, down Barra de Fero, the **Museu Europa d'Art Modern** (MEAM; www.meam.es) is a living museum which promotes figurative art from the late nineteenth century to the present day.

MANSIONS AND MUSEUMS

Barcelona's Institute of Culture champions the design world through museums, research and production. It encompasses

Stunning Palau de la Música Catalana

the much-vaunted **Museu del Disseny** (Design Museum; www.dissenyhub.barcelona) in Plaça de les Glòries, which hosts regular exhibitions and a permanent collection spanning fashion, textiles, product design and decorative arts. All the mansions along Carrer de Montcada merit a peek in at their courtyards, but one that's always open is the handsome Baroque **Palau Dalmases** (No. 20). On the ground floor is *Espai Barroc* ('Baroque Space'), an over-the-top, rococo bar. At the end of the street, in Plaçeta Montcada, you can feast on Basque tapas at *Euskal Etxea* (see page 119).

PALAU DE LA MÚSICA

Up Via Laietana, several blocks from Carrer Princesa, at Carrer del Palau de la Música 4–6, is one of the city's greatest achievements of *modernista* architecture, the **Palau de la Música Catalana** ⓬ (www.palaumusica.org). Designed by Lluís Domènech i Montaner, and built in 1908, it is the perfect expression of *modernisme* and a UNESCO World Heritage Site. It is an explosion of mosaics, tiles, stained glass, enamel, sculpture and carving. The brick exterior, with Moorish arches and columns inlaid with floral tiles, is sober compared to what's inside, where every square inch is embellished.

One of Domènech's main concerns was to let in as much natural light as possible, making the hall bright and airy. The structural skeleton is iron – an innovation in those days – which allows the walls to be made of glass. Sunlight streaming in during afternoon concerts sets the place ablaze. On either side of the stage the rich colours of the room are offset by sculpted groups of musical masters in white plaster. In between, the silvery pipes of a grand organ stand in orderly contrast. A curved wall is covered with mosaics of muses playing instruments; their upper bodies are made of porcelain and seem to emerge magically from the walls. Overhead is the Palau's crowning glory, a magical, stained-glass orb.

The best way to experience the Palau is to attend a concert. Programmes range from classical recitals to jazz (tel: 932 957 207). The alleyways opposite lead to Santa Caterina market, a dazzling renovation by architects EMTB – creators of the Scottish Parliament building – and a great place to eat.

EL EIXAMPLE

HIGHLIGHTS

» The Illa de la Discòrdia, see page 59
» Casa Batlló, see page 60
» La Pedrera, see page 60
» Passeig de Gràcia, see page 62
» Fundació Antoni Tàpies, see page 64
» La Sagrada Família, see page 65
» Gràcia and Park Güell, see page 67

The **Eixample** district, north of Plaça de Catalunya, is the city's main shopping and commercial area. You will probably want to spend a lot of time here if you are interested in Gaudí. The neighbourhood has spectacular apartment blocks, examples of early twentieth-century *modernista* architecture, and the central part is known as the **Quadrat d'Or** (Golden Square).

The principal avenues are the elegant Passeig de Gràcia and the Rambla de Catalunya, not to be confused with La Rambla. In a manageable area between the Gran Vía de les Corts Catalanes and Avinguda Diagonal, you'll find most of the *modernista* masterpieces. Barcelona's most-visited sight is Gaudí's unfinished cathedral, La Sagrada Família. On the northern outskirts of the Eixample, it can be easily reached on foot or by metro.

Passeig de Gràcia, one of the principal thoroughfares in Eixample

Despite the exuberance of the architecture, the city's 'modern' district is a model of rationalist urban planning, a rigid geometric grid simply called 'the Extension' *(Eixample)*. The outrageous and conservative coexist here without much fuss. Barcelona's expansion came about in a remarkable burst of urban development. By the mid-1800s the city was bursting at the seams and suffocating inside its ring of medieval walls. A competition was held in 1859 to select a plan for a new quarter between the old city and the Collserola hills. The

Passeig de Gràcia, a treasure trove of modernista architecture

job went to an engineer named Ildefons Cerdà, whose blueprint quintupled the city's size in a matter of decades. The Eixample construction transformed Barcelona into a showcase of extravagant *modernista* architecture, and the swanky Passeig de Gràcia became the place to be seen. Barcelona used the 1888 Universal Exposition as an open house to show the world its new face.

THE ILLA DE LA DISCÒRDIA

The best place to begin a *modernista* tour is on Passeig de Gràcia, with its single, hallucinatory block popularly known as the **Illa de la Discòrdia ⑱** (Block of Discord), set between Consell de Cent and Aragó. It gained its name because of the three stunning buildings in different architectural styles located almost next door to one other. At No. 35, Domènech i Montaner's impressive **Casa Lleó Morera** (1902–6) incorporates both Moorish and Gothic elements. This grand apartment house (www.casalleomorera.com) has suffered some disfigurement, especially on the ground floor, where the Spanish luxury brand Loewe installed picture windows and destroyed several original sculptures. Renovations happen quite regularly, so check before you go to ensure it is open. At No. 41 is the **Casa Amatller** (1900), built for a chocolate manufacturer. Puig i Cadafalch drew inspiration from Flanders for the stepped roof covered in glazed tiles. It is open to visitors (www.amatller.org). The caretaker's office has one of the finest stained-glass windows of the *modernista* era.

CASA BATLLÓ

Gaudí's highly personal **Casa Batlló** (1904–6) is next door and can be visited (www.casabatllo.es; book online as there is often a queue). The curvy contours, unexpected combinations of textures and materials, bright colours and infinite detail are Gaudí hallmarks, as are the prevalent religious and nationalist symbols. Casa Batlló is said to pay tribute to the patron saint of Catalonia, Sant Jordi, and the dragon he slayed. Gaudí himself left no clues as to his intent. The undulating blue-tile roof certainly looks like a dragon's scaly hide, while the balconies could be the skulls and bones of its victims (others have suggested they are Venetian carnival masks). Sant Jordi's cross and a shaft suggest a spear being thrust into the dragon's back. Its facade is covered with scraps of broken plate and tile, a decorative technique called *trencadís* that Gaudí employed repeatedly. In this case he dramatically remodelled both the exterior and interior of an existing house.

LA PEDRERA

Further up and across the street, at No. 92, is **Casa Milà** ⓮ (www.lapedrera.com) Gaudí's acclaimed apartment block. Known as **La Pedrera**

Curvy Casa Batlló

(the stone quarry, an allusion to its rippling, limestone surface), it was built between 1906 and 1910, and has been declared a UNESCO World Heritage Site. The sinuous facade, with wonderfully twisted wrought-iron balconies, bends around the corner of Carrer Provença.

The attic floor is now a handsome, high-tech museum (Espai Gaudí) sheltering an interesting exhibition of his work. One of the original apartments (El Pis) – all odd shapes, hand-crafted doorknobs and idiosyncratic details – has been outfitted with period furniture (many of the pieces designed by Gaudí himself), and can be visited.

La Pedrera had one of the world's first underground parking garages; today the space houses an amphitheatre where cultural conferences are held. The building's owner, the **Fundació Caixa de Catalunya**, has transformed the first floor into an exhibition space for impressively curated shows.

MODERNISME

Modernisme, a movement related to the design styles in vogue in Europe in the late nineteenth century – French Art Nouveau, German and Austrian Jugendstil – was a rebellion against the rigid forms and colourless stone and plaster of classical architecture. In Barcelona the new style assumed nationalist motifs and significance, which may be why it has been so carefully preserved here. Although there was an entire school of *modernista* architects working in Barcelona from the late nineteenth century until the 1930s, it is customary to speak of the 'Big Three': Antoni Gaudí, who left such a personal mark on the city; Lluís Domènech i Montaner (Palau de la Música Catalana and Casa Morera); and Josep Puig i Cadafalch (Casa Amatller, Casa Terrades and Els Quatre Gats), all of which are described in this Guide.

For many, the wavy rooftop is the highlight, with its decoration of recycled tiles, cluster of swirling Darth Vader-like chimneys known as 'witch scarers', and spectacular views of Barcelona.

PASSEIG DE GRÀCIA

You are likely to be busy peering up at decorative details or gazing in chic store windows along **Passeig de Gràcia**, but be sure to look down as well: Gaudí designed the hexagonal pavement tiles with nature motifs. The mosaic benches and iron streetlamps with little bat motifs (1900) are by Pere Falqués.

There are other numerous examples of *modernisme* throughout the Eixample. Duck down the streets that cut across Passeig de Gràcia, especially Diputació, Consell de Cent, Mallorca and València. In the Old Town you'll stumble across marvellous *modernista* store fronts, such as the stamp shop at Carrer dels Boters, the Antiga Casa Figueras pastry shop on the Ramblas and the wonderful dining room of the *Hotel España* in Carrer Sant Pau. Details of a special route, the Ruta del Modernisme, which takes in at least 115 examples, can be found online at www.rutadelmodernisme.com. In addition to the jewels of *modernista* architecture, Passeig de Gràcia and neighbouring Rambla Catalunya are lined with cafés, galleries, bookstores, boutiques and smart hotels. Daring enterprises like Casa Seat (Passeig de Gràcia 109), an all-in-one gallery, concert hall, co-working space and restaurant, naturally belong here. This is also the place for designer shopping, for both international and Spanish names like Adolfo Dominguez and Catalans Antonio Miró and Armand Basi, as well as high-street brands.

AROUND THE AVENUES

The **Plaça de Catalunya**, where Passeig de Gràcia begins, was designed to be the city's hub, and it is certainly a lively crossroads

Casa Milà, or La Pedrera, is a UNESCO World Heritage Site

and meeting place, especially the legendary *Café Zurich*. The bus, metro and the regional and national rail systems radiate from this square (see Transport, page 138) and El Corte Inglés department store occupies the whole of the northern side. Parallel to Passeig de Gràcia is the Rambla de Catalunya, an extension of the Old Town Rambles, peppered with smart shops, terrace cafés, restaurants and galleries. Traffic moves down either side of the pedestrianised centre, which is considerably more sedate than the lower Rambles.

On Carrer d'Aragó (between Passeig de Gràcia and Rambla Catalunya) is the **Fundació Antoni Tàpies** ⓯ (www.fundacio tapies.org), dedicated to the work of Catalonia – and perhaps Spain's – foremost contemporary artist (1923–2012). In addition to Tàpies' own work, it holds excellent temporary exhibitions, a study centre and library, and it is all housed in a gorgeous 1880 Domènech i Montaner building – one of the first examples of *modernisme*. From the outside, viewed from across the street, you can appreciate Tàpies' whimsical, tangled wire sculpture *Núvol i Cadira* (*Cloud and Chair*) on the roof.

ANTONI GAUDÍ

Count Eusebi Güell, a textile manufacturer, was Gaudí's patron and daring patron, a man who was able to accept the architect's wildly imaginative ideas. The Palau Güell, which Gaudí began in 1885 (see page 37), previews many aspects of his work. Gaudí died in 1926 at the age of 74, and is buried in the crypt of his great cathedral.

He was a deeply pious and conservative man, despite his innovations, and during his last years he lived in a room on the site, obsessed with the project. When passers-by discovered the architect run over by a tram in a nearby street in 1926 and took him to hospital, the doctors, unable at first to identify him, thought the dishevelled old man was an unhoused person. When it was discovered who he was, the entire city turned out for his funeral.

The iconic spires of the Sagrada Família

LA SAGRADA FAMÍLIA

What the Eiffel Tower is to Paris or the Statue of Liberty is to New York, the soaring spires of the **Sagrada Família** ⑯ (www.sagradafamilia. org; guided tours available daily) are to Barcelona. Its unmistakable profile, protruding from the city's skyline, is visible from afar. Yet the eight peculiar, cigar-shaped towers are merely the shell of a church that is nearing completion (now expected in 2026). This was Antoni Gaudí's life work, though he didn't really expect to finish it in his lifetime. Gaudí took over traditional, neo-Gothic plans of an earlier architect in 1883 and supervised work on the eastern, Nacimiento (Nativity) facade, one tower, and part of the apse and nave. This facade seems to be the one most faithful to Gaudí's intentions.

Everything has significance and no space is left unfilled. The three doorways, with stonework dripping like stalactites, represent

The Sagrada Família's soaring central nave

Faith, Hope and Charity, and are loaded with sculptures depicting angel choirs, musicians and Biblical episodes such as the birth of Jesus, the Flight into Egypt, the Slaughter of the Innocents, the Tree of Calvary, and much more. Twelve bell towers, four at each portal, will represent the Apostles; four higher towers, the Evangelists; a dome over the apse, the Virgin; and the central spire, which will be 170m (560ft), the Saviour.

For many years, the church remained much as it was when Gaudí died, but work has been going on since the 1950s – not an easy task, since Gaudí left few plans behind. Ascend one of the towers (by lift or spiral staircase) for an overview. The western Pasión facade (on Carrer de Sardenya), begun in 1952, includes controversial sculptures by Josep Maria Subirachs. Japanese sculptor Etsuro Sotoo's work can be seen on the Nacimiento facade.

Many people believe the temple should have been left as it was, unfinished, as a tribute to the great Gaudí, but the work continues, supervised by Jordi Bonet Armengol, the son of one of Gaudí's aides. In 2010 the central nave was finally covered, resplendent with its tree-like columns and dazzling roof, and the church was consecrated by Pope Benedict XVI.

A short walk along Avinguda de Gaudí is the **Hospital de la Santa Creu i Sant Pau** (www.santpaubarcelona.org), designed by

Domènech i Montaner. A working hospital until 2009, it is one of *modernisme*'s most underrated and least-known works and well worth visiting. A World Heritage Site, it houses part of the UN University and become an international centre for the Mediterranean.

GRÀCIA AND PARK GÜELL

Gràcia is a district above the Eixample, retaining a village atmosphere with small, independent local shops and its own town square, Plaça de la Vila de Gràcia (formerly Plaça Rius i Taulet). Streets named Llibertat and Fraternitat and a Plaça Revolució nod to a politically charged past. Gràcia is a popular nightspot, known for its *Festa Major*, which runs for seven days starting from around 15 August. On the hills behind Gràcia, **Park Güell** ⓱ (www.

Gaudí's much-loved Park Güell

The marina at Port Vell

parkguell.barcelona/en), another wildly ambitious Gaudí project, was planned as a residential community, to be intertwined with nature. Gaudí's patron, Eusebi Güell, bought six hectares (fifteen acres) here, overlooking the city and the sea, intending to create a kind of English garden suburb. He gave Gaudí carte blanche to produce something original, and for the next fourteen years, on and off, the architect let his imagination run wild; much of the design was, however, eventually completed by Josep Maria Jujol.

Two gingerbread pavilions guard the entrance on Carrer d'Olot: the one on the left is a shop, the one on the right an exhibition centre. In front of them is a tiled lizard fountain; supporting columns mimic tree trunks. Ceilings are decorated with fragments of plates, and undulating benches are splashed with colourful ceramic pieces, known as *trencadís*. Beneath the plaza is the **Saló**

de les Cent Columnes (Hall of the One Hundred Columns). There are actually 86, Doric in style, in what was to be the colony's covered market. Dolls' heads, bottles, glasses and plates are stuck in the ceiling mosaics. Only five buildings were completed, one of which Gaudí lived in for many years, now the **Casa-Museu Gaudí** (www.casamuseugaudi.org), a museum of his furniture and memorabilia.

THE WATERFRONT

HIGHLIGHTS

- » Museu Marítim, see page 70
- » Port Vell, see page 70
- » Barceloneta, see page 71
- » Olympic Village and beyond, see page 72
- » Parc de la Ciutadella, see page 73

Barcelona turned its back on the sea during the nineteenth century and focused on developing industry. The sea wall where families loved to walk and catch the breeze on stifling summer nights was dismantled. Access to the water was obstructed by warehouses and railway tracks, and expansion marched towards the hills. Barceloneta, a neighbourhood created in the early eighteenth century between the port and the beach as part of a military initiative, remained a close-knit working-class community. However, things changed with the development of an ambitious recreational and commercial area along the waterfront in the early 1990s.

NOTES

A perennial waterfront attraction are the ferries called Golondrinas (Swallows; www.lasgolondrinas.com), moored opposite the Columbus Monument. These boats have been taking passengers round the harbour ever since the 1888 World Exposition.

MARITIME HERITAGE

Begin a tour of the waterfront at the Columbus Monument, at the foot of the Ramblas. To the right is **Les Reials Drassanes**, begun in 1255, and now housing the beautifully renovated **Museu Marítim** ⑱ (www.mmb.cat). The sixteen bays of these great shipyards, which handled more than thirty galleys, launched ships that extended Catalonia's dominion over the Mediterranean from Tunis to Greece, Sicily, Sardinia and much of the French coast. The museum contains models from the earliest galleys to the cargo and passenger vessels that have made Barcelona their home port. The prize exhibit is a full-size copy of Don Juan of Austria's victorious flagship *La Galera Reial*.

PORT VELL

At the other side of the busy Passeig de Colom is an undulating wooden walkway and footbridge called the **Rambla del Mar**, which stretches across the mouth of the **Port Vell**. It crosses over to the Moll d'Espanya and **Maremàgnum**, packed with shops, bars and restaurants – some with terraces overlooking the harbour. Families head for **L'Aquàrium** ⑲ (www.aquariumbcn.com), one of Europe's largest. A spectacular glass tunnel running through its huge oceanarium allows visitors to walk beneath the water for over eighty metres with only a few inches of glass separating them from the sharks and other sea life above.

The port is busy with yachts, cruise ships and ferries to Mallorca and Italy. Overhead, cable cars link Montjuïc with the Torre de Jaume I and the Torre de Sant Sebastià in Barceloneta. The **World Trade Center**, a hotel and complex of offices designed by I.M. Pei, appears to be floating in the harbour.

On the mainland, the **Moll de la Fusta**, the old wood-loading quay, was transformed into a promenade in the 1980s, and redesigned and landscaped after the 1992 Olympics. Where the Moll d'Espanya joins the promenade, look out for colourful surrealist sculpture **Barcelona Head** (*El Cap de Barcelona*) by American artist Roy Lichtenstein.

The Platja Barceloneta in full swing

Heading towards Barceloneta you skirt the **Marina Port Vell**, a harbour for luxury yachts and chic motor cruisers. On the **Moll de Barceloneta**, in a stylishly renovated warehouse complex, the Palau de Mar houses the **Museu d'Història de Catalunya ⑳** (www.mhcat.cat), which is fun as well as informative. A rooftop bar with a stunning view is on the top floor. Along the Passeig Joan de Borbó, which runs parallel to the quay, numerous popular restaurants have outside tables.

BARCELONETA

If you want to eat caught-that-day fish, head to Barceloneta, a district for many years separated from the city in spirit as well as by physical barriers of water and rail yards. It was built in the early eighteenth century to house dispossessed families when La Ribera was demolished to make way for the Ciutadella fortress. A robust *barrio* inhabited by fishermen's families, its beaches were scruffy and dominated by flimsy wooden restaurant shacks (*chiringuitos*).

When the area was virtually rebuilt in preparation for the 1992 Olympics, the *chiringuitos* were wiped out, and many Barceloneses nostalgically mourn their loss. You can cut through the grid of narrow streets or walk along the beach to the **Passeig Marítim** and the landscaped promenade running alongside the wooden walkways and scrupulously clean sands of **Platja Barceloneta**.

OLYMPIC VILLAGE AND BEYOND

Keep walking and you will come to the 1992 Olympic Village, the **Vila Olímpica**, an award-winning development that has

Museu Blau

blossomed into a smart and vibrant neighbourhood. It is recognisable from afar by two high-rise buildings – one the prestigious *Hotel Arts* – and Frank Gehry's enormous, shimmering copper fish.

Parc de la Ciutadella

As you approach, passing a small park, the gleaming Hospital de Mar and a *modernista* water tower, the promenade here and in the **Port Olímpic** just beyond becomes increasingly crowded with bars, cafés and restaurants.

Beyond the Olympic Port, a line of metal poles follows a path inland to the Poble Nou district, known for its textile production. Today the factories have been reimagined as design studios, office blocks and apartments, and gentrification continues, spreading north and west to meet Avinguda Diagonal.

At the end of the seafront promenade, **Diagonal Mar** and the Parc del Fòrum have formed a hi-tech residential and commercial neighbourhood. The landmark triangular Forum Building is home to the **Museu Blau** ㉑ (Blue Museum; http://museuciencies.cat), an interactive natural history and science museum which offers temporary exhibits at the museum and the Botanical Garden.

PARC DE LA CIUTADELLA

Lodged between the Olympic Village and La Ribera is **Parc de la Ciutadella** ㉒ the city's largest park which incorporates the zoo, the **Parc Zoológic** (www.zoobarcelona.cat). This was the site, first, of the fortress built after the fall of Barcelona in 1714, and then of the 1888 World Exposition. Housed in a splendid *modernista* building designed for this event is the **Laboratori de Natura**, a branch of the Natural Science Museum (http://museuciencies.cat/en) housing its library and research centre. Nearby stands the Museu Martorell, which used to shelter the geological collection. Now it's yet another branch of the Natural Science Museum, which features the 'Land of Dragons' – a recreation of the natural habitat of the komodo dragon, with panoramic views of the huge reptiles from various viewing points.

The popular park is always a refuge from the intensity of the city's streets. There's a lake where rowing boats can be hired, and shady benches beneath towering trees filled with parakeets. The large Baroque fountain, **La Cascada**, was designed by Josep Fontseré, whose assistant was a young architecture student named Antoni Gaudí. In the Plaça d'Armes is the Parlament de Catalunya. The autonomous government debates the issues of the day in a handsome building, once the arsenal of the eighteenth-century citadel. From the park's exit on Pujades, a broad promenade sweeps up to the imposing **Arc de Triomf**, built as the entrance to the 1888 Exposition. To the right, near university buildings on Wellington, a tram can be caught to Diagonal Mar. On the sea side of the park lies the grand Estació de França railway station, and along Avinguda Marquès de l'Argentera is **La Llotja**, a centre of Barcelona's trading activities for more than six hundred years and former Stock Exchange. It is a handsome building with an attractive courtyard and a fourteenth-century Gothic hall.

Almost opposite is the splendid arcade of **Porxos Xifré**, a nineteenth-century complex that houses the **Restaurant 7 Portes** (http://7portes.com/en), a Barcelona institution (see page 123). If you head back towards the Rambla past the city's monumental Correus (Post Office), along Passeig de Colom, you will pass the

Baroque splendour of the **Mare de Déu de la Mercè**. The church is best known for the sculpture of the Madonna on its dome, which can be seen for miles around and is something of a local landmark.

EL RAVAL

HIGHLIGHTS

» Museu d'Art Contemporani de Barcelona, see page 76
» Centre de Cultura Contemporània de Barcelona, see page 76

The district between La Rambla, the Ronda de Sant Antoni and Paral.lel is **El Raval**, where numerous buildings have been demolished to create urban spaces and new housing. From La

'48 Portraits' by Gerhard, MACBA

La Rambla, take Carrer del Carme, then turn right up Carrer dels Àngels to reach the most conspicuous symbol of this neighbourhood's transformation: Richard Meier's **MACBA**, or **Museu d'Art Contemporani de Barcelona** ㉓ (www.macba. es). The museum is worth visiting for its architecture and the multicultural buzz in its square, where skateboarders, art lovers and locals all congregate. It has some fine abstract works and good temporary exhibitions. Next door is the ever-stimulating **Centre de Cultura Contemporània de Barcelona** (www.cccb.org), a striking renovation of the Casa de Caritat. In this exciting space, dance, music, film and other activities explore the urban experience.

Retrace your steps to Carrer del Carme and the Gothic complex of the **Antic Hospital de la Santa Creu** (Hospital of the Holy Cross), a hospital and refuge for pilgrims for a thousand years. Gaudí died here in 1926. The present structures were begun in 1401. Look for the frieze of sixteenth-century tiles on the life of St Paul in the entryway of the Institut d'Estudis Catalans. The courtyard is restful, with benches beneath orange trees ripe with fruit or fragrant with blossom. The Escola Massana Art School, the National Library of Catalonia, and the Institute for Catalan Studies are all housed here.

URBAN REGENERATION

Carrer Hospital is a busy commercial street studded with trendy little shops and restaurants, though the narrow alleys shooting off the thoroughfare are best avoided. Check out Rieva Baixa for vintage shops, and the recently created Rambla del Raval. Old housing was demolished to make way for it, and new blocks and a towering five-star hotel are all part of the urban regeneration process that is attracting a bohemian crowd.

Around the corner is a Romanesque gem, the little church of **Sant Pau del Camp** (www.santpaudelcamp.info). The simplicity of its twelfth-century lines is an agreeable change from the extravagance of Barcelona's *modernisme* and the intricacies of

Plaça d'Espanya, Montjuïc

Gothic architecture. It is believed to be the oldest church in the city. The lovely little cloister has Arab-style arches.

MONTJUÏC

HIGHLIGHTS

» Museu Nacional d'Art de Catalunya, see page 79
» Fundació Joan Miró, see page 80
» Poble Espanyol, see page 82

Montjuïc came into its own as the site of Barcelona's 1929 International Exhibition, and again for the 1992 Olympic Games. It has since been rejuvenated so its shady gardens, 210-metre (689ft) summit, panoramic views and outstanding complex of museums and sports facilities are more popular than ever. The Plaça d'Espanya is a good point to begin a visit to Montjuïc, as it has a metro and bus stop. If you'd rather the more scenic route you can take the cable car directly to the castle.

Beside the square is a bullring built in 1899, now home to the **Arenas de Barcelona**, a shopping, cultural and recreational facility. A central avenue leads upwards to the vast **Palau Nacional**, which shelters the Catalan art museum, MNAC, and past the **Font Màgica** ❷ (Magic Fountain), which performs a *son et lumière* show. Nearby is the seminal **Pavelló Mies van der Rohe** (www.miesbcn.com), built for the 1929 Exposition, dismantled, then rebuilt in 1986. The glass, stone and steel cube house is a wonder of cool Bauhaus forms.

The frescoed dome of the Palau Nacional

Opposite is **Casaramona**, a magnificent *modernista* textile factory converted into the **CaixaForum** (https://obrasociallacaixa.org), the Fundació la Caixa's wonderful cultural centre, with a full programme of exhibitions and concerts.

CATALAN ART TREASURES

External lifts make the ascent to the domed Palau Nacional easier. This is the **Museu Nacional d'Art de Catalunya** ㉕ (www.museunacional.cat), housing one of the world's finest collections of Romanesque art. Another building constructed for the 1929 Exposition, it holds a thousand years of Catalan art, bringing together various collections under one roof, including part of the Thyssen-Bornemisza display, and the nineteenth- and twentieth-century curation of the former Museu d'Art Modern de Catalunya. It also holds excellent temporary exhibitions.

Between the ninth and thirteenth centuries, over two thousand Romanesque churches were built in Catalonia. Interiors were decorated with painted altar panels, carved wooden crosses, Madonnas of great purity and primitive sculptures of biblical episodes or rural life on the capitals of columns. At the start of the twentieth century, many works were saved from deteriorating in abandoned churches and are now displayed in the museum. There are masterpieces in every room.

The Gothic wing is excellent, too. Many of the paintings are retablos, screens with arched frames that stood behind chapel altars.

NOTES

A funicular from Avinguda del Paral.lel metro station runs to Avinguda de Miramar (near the Fundació Joan Miró), and links up with the Telefèric, the cable car that gives a ride with a view up to the Castell de Montjuïc. Another cable car, the Transbordador Aéri, shuttles passengers from Montjuïc right across the port to Barceloneta, stopping at the World Trade Center.

Among the treasures are Lluís Dalmau's painting, *Virgin of the Councillors* (1445); Jaume Ferrer II's altarpiece St Jerome; and a fine retable of St John the Baptist with saints Sebastian and Nicholas.

The nineteenth- and twentieth-century gallery includes works by Casas, Fortuny, Mir, Nonell and Rusiñol. Displays have been further enhanced with a selection of paintings by Barcelona-born Carmen Thyssen-Bornemisza.

MUSEUMS AND MIRÓ

Up the hill is the **Museu d'Arqueologia de Catalunya** ㉖ (www. mac.cat). Among the exhibits, drawn mainly from prehistoric, Iberian, Greek and Roman sites in Catalonia, are reconstructions of tombs and life-like dioramas.

The Anella Olímpica (Olympic Ring), Montjuïc

Further up lie the Jardins de Laribal, fringed by the **Teatre Grec** amphitheatre, where the Festival Grec is held in summer. Steps from here lead to **Fundació Joan Miró** ㉗ (www.fmirobcn.org), an excellent museum designed by the architect Josep Lluís Sert to house a large collection of paintings, drawings, tapestries and sculpture by the Catalan surrealist, who died in 1983 at 90. The exhibits follow Miró's artistic development from 1914 onwards. In the grounds outside is a smattering of his sculptures.

The **Castell de Montjuïc** (www.ajuntament.barcelona.

Miró sculpture outside the Fundació Joan Miró

cat/castelldemontjuic/en), built in 1640, remained in use by the army, then as a prison until shortly before it was turned over to the city in 1960. The fort has sombre associations for the city: its cannons bombarded the population to crush rebellions in the eighteenth and nineteenth centuries, and it was the site of political executions. The **Jardí Botànic** (www.museuciencies.bcn.cat), between the Olympic Stadium and the castle, is a sustainable garden showcasing plants from across the Mediterranean.

The **Anella Olímpica** (Olympic Ring) spreads across the northern side of Montjuïc and can be reached by escalator from the Palau Nacional. The original 1929 Estadi Olímpic (Olympic stadium) was enlarged for the 1992 Games and improved for the European Athletics Championships in 2010. Near the entrance to the stadium is **Museu Olímpic i de l'Esport** ❷❽ (www.museuolimpicbcn.

cat), a must for sports enthusiasts. Just beyond is the high-tech **Palau Sant Jordi** sports stadium, designed by Japanese architect Arata Isozaki. It can seat 17,000 spectators beneath a 45-metre (148ft) roof. Towering over it all is the 188-metre (616ft) **Torre de Calatrava** communications tower.

POBLE ESPANYOL

Down the hill is the **Poble Espanyol** ㉙ (Spanish Village; www. poble-espanyol.com), a family attraction by day and a popular nightspot after dark. Built for the 1929 Exposition, it's a composite of architecture representing Spain's varied regions, including replicas of houses, church towers, fountains, plazas and palaces strung along a network of streets and squares. The entrance is through a gate of the walled city of Ávila. There is a flamenco show, restaurants, discos and demonstrations of regional crafts, including weaving, pottery and glassblowing, which make it a good place to find well-made souvenirs.

THE DIAGONAL

HIGHLIGHT

» Pedralbes, see page 83

The broad Avinguda Diagonal slices across Cerdà's grid from the coast to the hills linking up with the city ring roads. From Diagonal Mar a tram runs through **22@ district** ㉚, with its cutting-edge architecture, up to the busy Plaça de les Glòries Catalanes roundabout. Jean Nouvel's gherkin-like **Torre Glòries** spectacularly marks the spot, illuminated at night by 4500 glass panels. Formerly known as Torre Agbar, it's the Spanish HQ for Facebook owners Meta. Tickets are available for the observation deck, which includes an interactive climbing frame, so you can soar to even greater heights. Nearby is the state-of-the-art **Museu del Disseny**

El Sagrat Cor

(www.dissenyhub.barcelona/en), whose 70,000 objects exemplify the best of Catalan design through the ages. Nearby is Ricardo Bofill's Neoclassical **Teatre Nacional de Catalunya** and Rafael Moneo's **L'Auditori**, a concert hall which includes the **Museu de la Música** (http://w110.bcn.cat).

PEDRALBES

Further up the Diagonal is the **Palau de Pedralbes**, a Güell-family estate converted into a royal residence in 1919. On the other side of the Diagonal is the Zona Universitària and **Camp Nou Stadium**, home of Barcelona's revered football club, Barça, with a museum that includes a tour (www.fcbarcelona.com).

At the top of Avinguda de Pedralbes is the atmospheric **Monestir de Pedralbes** ❸ (www.monestirpedralbes.bcn.cat).

Founded in 1326 by Queen Elisenda de Montcada, whose tomb is in the superb Gothic church, it has a beautiful three-storey cloister.

The districts on the hillsides were once separate villages where residents of Barcelona spent summers and weekends. They've been absorbed over the years, but each preserves its own character. Pedralbes is patrician – expensive villas with gardens – while Sarrià retains the feel of a small, charming Catalan town.

TIBIDABO

The first bright, clear morning or late afternoon of your visit, head for **Tibidabo** ㉜, the 512-metre (1680ft) peak of the Collserola range, overlooking the city. The views are breathtaking. The church of **El Sagrat Cor**, floodlit at night, built in the first half of the twentieth century in neo-Romanesque and neo-Gothic style, and surmounted by a monumental figure of Christ, is one of the city's landmarks.

To reach the summit, take the FGC train from the Plaça de Catalunya to Avda Tibidabo. From here the **Tramvia Blau**, an old-fashioned blue wooden tram runs every day during the summer, taking you up to the funicular station. Don't miss the nearby **CosmoCaixa** (www.cosmocaixa.org/es), a splendid science museum with a planetarium that projects a 3D show using the latest technology.

Nearby is Torre Bellesguard (Casa Figueras; www.bellesguardgaudi.com) – Antonio Gaudí's most personal project. Next to a crumbling 500-year-old medieval castle, the residence has an impressive tower was designed in the neo-Gothic style in 1900–1909.

From Plaça del Dr Andreu the funicular glides through pine woods to the top, where you have a spectacular panorama of the city, the coast and the Pyrenees. Families flock to the popular 1950s-style amusement park, the **Parc d'Atraccions** (www.tibidabo.cat). With over 25 attractions, many of the old favourites remain but there is now a new generation of thrilling modern rides to experience, too. Check out the Sky Walk, an area with some of the best views of Barcelona.

The **Parc de Collserola** is a huge, green swathe that makes a great escape from the city. Families come here at weekends and summer evenings to enjoy the fresh air. There are jogging and cycling tracks, nature trails, picnic spots and *merenderos*, where you barbecue your own food.

Another high spot is the **Torre de Collserola** communications tower (www.torredecollserola.com), designed by Sir Norman Foster for the 1992 Barcelona Olympics. A transparent lift whisks you to the top for fabulous panoramic views.

EXCURSIONS

HIGHLIGHTS

There's a great deal to detain you in Barcelona, but just beyond the city are several sites eminently worthy of day-trips. These include the holy Catalan shrine of Montserrat, the relaxed and pretty town of Sitges for beaches and museums, and the cava wine country in the region of Penedès.

Montserrat's paths are studded with sculptures

MONTSERRAT

Montserrat ㉝ (www.montserratvisita.com), Catalonia's most important religious retreat and the shrine of Catalan nationhood, rises out of the rather featureless Llobregat plain 48km (thirty miles) northwest of Barcelona. The view from its 1241-metre (4075ft) summit can take in both the Pyrenees and Mallorca, and the monastery itself can be seen from afar, surrounded by the jagged ridges that give it its name – the Serrated Mountain.

The first hermitages on the mountain may have been established by those trying to escape the Moorish invasion. One was enlarged as a Benedictine monastery in the eleventh century and a century later it became the repository for **La Moreneta**, the Black Madonna, a small, wooden image of a Virgin (darkened by candle smoke) holding the infant Jesus on her lap and a globe in her right hand. The figure is said to be a carving by St Luke, later hidden by St Peter. Ever since, pilgrims – from commoners to kings – have climbed the mountain to worship the Catalan patron saint. More than a million pilgrims and tourists visit the shrine each year.

The **monastery** was burned to the ground by Napoleon's soldiers in 1808, abandoned in 1835 when all convents were sequestered by the state, and rebuilt in 1874. During the Spanish Civil War, La Moreneta was secretly replaced by a copy; the original remained hidden during the dictatorship. Although Catalan culture was suppressed, monks here continued to say Mass in Catalan.

The site of the monastery is spectacular, tucked into folds of rock high above the plain. On the eve of the saint's day, 27 April, the monks hold an all-night vigil attended by huge crowds. La Moreneta gazes down from a gold-and-glass case, above and to the right of the altar in the **basilica**, but the faithful can touch or kiss her right hand through an opening. Each day the Escolans, the oldest boys' choir in Europe, founded in the thirteenth century, fill the basilica with their pure voices. The monastery and its underground **museum** conceal many valuable works of art, including paintings by El Greco.

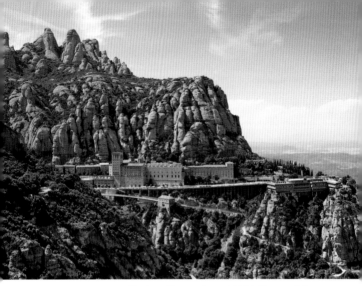

Montserrat's monastery, set high in the mountains

Montserrat is also popular with cyclists and mountain climbers who ascend the spires of rock above the building. From the monastery there are walks to other hermitages and a funicular to the **Santa Cova**, the cave sacred to the legend of the Madonna. Statues and plaques stud the paths.

Due to its popularity, Montserrat has a cluster of bars, restaurants and shops around the Plaça de la Creu. For a peaceful visit, spend the night in the hotel or former monks' cells.

Getting there

Montserrat can be reached in an hour by FGC train from Barcelona's Plaça d'Espanya to either Montserrat Aeri, where a cable car continues up the side of the mountain to the monastery, or the next stop, Monistrol de Montserrat, where the more comfortable Cremallera train trundles up to the monastery, for the same price. If you are driving, leave Barcelona via the Diagonal and hit the A2 highway in the direction of Lleida, taking the exit to Manresa for Monistrol.

SITGES

It's easy to get to the Costa Daurada beaches from Barcelona. The coast south of the city earned its name from its broad, golden sands, in contrast to the rocky coves of the Costa Brava to the north. **Sitges** ㉞, a favourite resort (www.visitsitges.com) of Barceloneses, is the best place for a day-trip. It's a short drive on the R2 motorway, or a forty-minute train ride from Sants or Passeig de Gràcia stations, if you board a fast train – some of the slower services stop frequently en route. There is also a scenic coastal drive, which is narrow and curvy and takes longer.

Happily, the pretty little town has escaped the high-rises and tawdry atmosphere of many coastal resorts, although it does get somewhat overwhelmed by crowds in summer. It is a popular spot with the LGBTQ+ crowd. There are two beaches, separated by a promontory where gleaming, whitewashed houses hook around the church of **Sant Bartolomeu i Santa Tecla**. The biggest and best beach is **Platja d'Or** so named for its golden sands, backed by a palm-lined promenade and dozens of cafés and restaurants – some of them very good indeed. North of the promontory is Sant Sebastià beach, smaller, quieter and extremely pleasant.

Three seaside museums

Besides the beaches, Sitges is known for its appealing museums. The **Museu Cau Ferrat** (www.museusdesitges.cat) occupies the house built by the painter Santiago Rusiñol (1861–1931), whose collection of works by El Greco, Casas, Picasso and others is on display, along with many of his own works.

Next to Cau Ferrat is the **Museu Maricel** (www.museusdesitges. cat/en), a splendid house overlooking the foam-tipped waves – the name means 'sea and sky'. It displays a small curation of Gothic sculpture and paintings, some notable murals by Josep Maria Sert (1876–1945) and the town's art collection, with paintings by the Romantics, Lumanists and Modernists.

The outskirts of Sitges are dotted with the grand villas of wealthy Barceloneses, while the pretty streets between the beach and station are geared for food and fun. Sitges has one of Spain's largest LGBTQ+ communities, and attracts queer travellers year-round, but particularly during the riotous February carnival. Gay and nudist beaches lie a little way beyond town.

Located inland from Sitges, on the road to Vilafranca, is **Sant Pere de Ribes**, which has a tenth-century castle and a delightful Romanesque church.

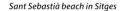

Sant Sebastià beach in Sitges

SANT SADURNÍ D'ANOIA (PENEDÈS)

Cava, Catalonia's sparkling wine, comes from **Penedès**, a pretty region south of Barcelona (45min on the train from Sants or Plaça de Catalunya; by road, take the AP7 in the direction of Tarragona). These days the top-selling cavas are produced by Codorníu and Freixenet. The centre of production is the small town of **Sant Sadurní d'Anoia** ❸❺, where several wineries offer guided tours and tastings.

The most interesting of these is **Codorníu** (www.codorniu.com), Spain's largest producer of cava. In business since 1872, the family-owned winery is spread across a spectacular campus, with *modernista* buildings by Gaudí's contemporary, Puig i Cadafalch. Completed in 1898, it has been declared a National Artistic and Historic Monument. Visitors to the winery are taken on a theme-park-like ride

Basílica de Santa Maria in Vilafranca del Penedès

through 26km (sixteen miles) of underground cellars.

World-famous cava producer **Freixenet** has its headquarters next to the station (www.freixenet.es).

There is a clutch of good restaurants in and near town, which the staff at Codorníu will be happy to tell you about. Most of them specialise in seafood paired, of course, with cava. If you visit between January and March you must try another regional dish, *calçots* – baby leeks grilled and dipped in a peppery, garlicky sauce – so popular they actually have a fiesta in their honour at this time, called the *calçotada*.

Fiesta celebrations in Vilafranca del Penedès

VILAFRANCA DEL PENEDÈS

Some fifteen kilometres (eight miles) to the south of Sant Sadurní, surrounded by vineyards, is the town of **Vilafranca del Penedès** ㊱, the capital of the Alt-Penedès region and the place behind the world-renowned Torres red wine.

The **Vinseum: Museu de les Cultures del Vi de Catalunya** (www. vinseum.cat) is reputed to be one of the best wine museums in Europe. It is housed in the renovated Gothic **Palau Reial**, residence of the count-kings of Barcelona-Aragón. The local festival (29 August–2 September), when the wine flows freely and the human towers called *castells* make their appearance, is a good time to visit the tow.

Teatre Lliure, one of Barcelona's temples to culture

Things to do

As you would expect from a city of its size, Barcelona has a busy arts and culture calendar – there will always be something worth catching, whether it's a contemporary dance performance, cabaret show or night at the opera. Almost any month you choose to visit Barcelona you'll coincide with a saint's day, festival or holiday. Traditionally, each neighbourhood celebrates with its own festa, though the major ones – like Sants' and Gràcia's Festa Majors and the Mercè – have become city institutions. Meanwhile, biggest and best of the annual arts and music events are the summer Festival de Barcelona Grec, the ever-expanding Sónar extravaganza of electronic music and multimedia art, and the rock and indie fest that is Primavera Sound.

If you prefer running to raving, join locals jogging or hiking in the surrounding hills of the Parc del Collserola. Barcelona is well placed for access to the sea and mountains, which is one of the reasons it was picked for the 1992 Olympics. In addition, there are scores of sports centres and swimming pools throughout the city.

CULTURE

A concert at the **Palau de la Música** (Carrer del Palau de la Música 4–6, www.palaumusica.cat), the *modernista* masterpiece, is a wonderful experience, whatever the performance. The varied programme includes chamber and symphony concerts, contemporary music and occasionally jazz.

Barcelona's famous opera house, **Gran Teatre del Liceu** (La Rambla 51–59, www.liceubarcelona.cat), which was gutted by fire in 1994, reopened to general acclaim in 1999. It hosts extravagant and avant-garde productions and a short ballet season. Tickets are hard to score, despite its increased seating capacity, but worth a try. **L'Auditori** (Plaça de les Arts), home of the OBC (Barcelona Symphony Orchestra), has a 2500-seat auditorium and a smaller one for chamber concerts (www.auditori.cat). The **CaixaForum** (Av. de Francesc Ferrer I Guàrdia 6–8) is a sophisticated cultural centre that hosts musical performances as well as exhibitions and other events.

The **Teatre Nacional de Catalunya** (Plaça de les Arts, www.tnc.cat) has a wide and varied programme, and the **Teatre Lliure** (Passeig de Santa Madrona, www.teatrelliure.com) stages good contemporary productions. Most productions are in Catalan, occasionally Spanish, and foreign companies visit at festival time. The **Mercat de les Flors** (Lleida 59, http://mercatflors.cat) specialises in dance and movement.

Tickets for cultural events can be booked at the information centre in Palau Virreina on La Rambla and at the venue's box office.

Harlem Jazz Club

NIGHTLIFE

For seasoned *juerguistas* (ravers) the Barcelona nightlife is hard to beat. For early evening don't miss atmospheric cocktail bars **Boadas** (Tallers 1) and long-established **Dry Martini** (Aribau 162). The more traditional **Bodega Cal Marino** (Carrer de Margarit 54; www.calmarino.com) sells wines from the barrel to drink in its stone-walled tavern or take away at knockdown prices. Add cheap tapas and a jolly neighbourhood crowd, and there are more than enough reasons to stop by.

The scene really hots up after midnight, much of it centred on the Old Town, where a few remnants of the old Barri Xino mingle with hip nightspots and restaurants that are open for drinks into the small hours. Meanwhile, the bulk of the big-name warehouse and designer venues are in peripheral areas such as Poblenou and Les Corts. Also high on the list of any seasoned clubber is **La Terrrazza** (www.laterrrazza.com) in Poble Espanyol, Montjuïc. The Born area is cool for classics like **Gimlet** (Santaló 46) or **Berimbau** (Passeig del Born 17), while the Plaça Reial in the Barri Gòtic drums to every kind of beat from disco **Karma** (www.karma disco.com) to the iconic **Jamboree** (www.jamboreejazz.com/en), which has hosted live jazz, blue and funk nights since the 1960s.

> **NOTES**
>
> *Resident Advisor* (www.ra.co/events/es/barcelona) runs the gamut of nightlife listings in Barcelona while the *Metropolitan* has previews, reviews and articles in English (www.barcelona-metropolitan.com).

Uptown, **Bling Bling** (Carrer de Tuset 10, http://blingblingbcn.com), **Sala Apolo** (Nou de la Rambla 113, www.sala-apolo.com) and **Razzmatazz** (Pamplona 88, www.salarazzmatazz.com) are the top spots in town. In summer the *chiringuitos* on every beach from Barceloneta to Diagonal Mar are packed with dancers till dawn.

FESTIVALS AND EVENTS

Barcelona's music festivals are diverse and spread out across the year: **Festival de Guitarra de Barcelona** (www.theproject.es) in March, the **Festival Internacional de Jazz** (www.jazz.barcelona) in October and November, and the **Grec Summer Festival** of dance, music and theatre (http://lameva.barcelona.cat/grec/en) in July. Events are held all over the city, but the most impressive are at the **Grec Theatre**, an open-air amphitheatre on Montjuïc (check programme and buy tickets at the Virreina Palace, La Rambla 99; see page 34).

Usually held in the second or third week of June, **Sónar** (www. sonar.es) is Europe's biggest and most cutting-edge electronic music, multimedia and urban art festival, attracting over 100,000 visitors to its three-day extravaganza of brilliant noise and spectacle. Sónar by day centres on events at Fira Montjuïc; after dark the action shifts to L'Hospitalet, with all-night buses running from the city to the bars and clubs.

If you're in the city during a festival, you'll see the different neighbourhoods erupt into life. Food, fireworks, music and the huge papier-mâché effigies called *gegants* (giants) and their companions, the *cap grossos* (bigheads), are essential features. The *gegants* are about four metres (13ft) high and elaborately dressed as kings and queens, knights and ladies. *Cap grossos* are cartoon heads of

Human castles at La Mercè Festival

well-known personalities, often with *dracs* (dragons) and *dimonis* (devils).

A constant of Catalan festivals are the *castellers*, acrobatic troupes who form human towers up to nine people high. This takes place most spectacularly at **La Mercè Festival**, on 24 September (festivities begin a few days before), in the Plaça de Sant Jaume. The **pre-Lent Carnaval** is another excuse to dress up and hold processions and parties. Like most festivals it is accompanied by late-night bands and plenty of fireworks (see page 100).

La Liga match at the Camp Nou stadium

SPORTS AND OUTDOOR ACTIVITIES

Barcelona is well placed for access to the sea and mountains, which is one of the reasons it was picked for the 1992 Olympics – the event that really put the modern city on the map. A spin-off from the games was an increased provision of top-quality sports and leisure facilities throughout Catalunya, which have attracted an increasing number of major games events, such as the European Athletics Championships, the IAAF World Junior Championships, the World Swimming Championships, the UEFA Champions League finals and the Americas Cup. Most residents are active outdoor enthusiasts, eager to escape the city for cycling, sailing or skiing, the latter only a couple of hours away in the Pyrenees.

FOOTBALL

The great spectator sport in Barcelona is football, and a match involving Barça (www.fcbarcelona.com), one of Europe's perennial champions, can bring the city to a standstill. The club's **Camp Nou** stadium, in the Les Corts area near the Diagonal, is the largest in Europe. Camp Nou has one of the most-visited museums in Spain (check website for details). Match tickets can be purchased ahead online at the club's website or on the day at the ticket office on Travessera de les Corts, though seats can be scarce for big matches.

The city does have another football club, Espanyol, who are based at the **RCDE stadium** in the suburb of Cornella de Llobregat; match tickets for their games are easier to get hold of (www.rcdespanyol.com).

CYCLING

Cycling is popular and tourist offices can provide a map showing recommended routes and bike lanes and offer advice about taking bikes on public transport. Alternatively, contact **Amics de la Bici** (Demóstenes 19, www.amicsdelabici.org). On Tibidabo, the **Carretera de las Aiguas**, a scenic path that winds along the mountain with spectacular views of the city below, is a great place to walk, jog or cycle. **Barcelona by Bike** offers easy-going cycling tours around the city (www.barcelonabybike.com). Bikes can be rented from **Biciclot** (Pere IV, 58, www.biciclot.coop), where there is easy access to the Parc de la Ciutadella and the waterfront (tandems and child seats available).

GOLF

The **Reial Club de Golf El Prat** (El Prat de Llobregat, www.realclub degolfelprat.com) offers 45 holes designed by golfing legend Greg Norman. Clubs and carts can be hired, and there's a swimming pool for non-participants. Other courses located nearby include **Club de Golf Sant Cugat** (Sant Cugat del Vallès; www.golfsantcugat.

com), just west of the city, which hires out clubs and trolleys and has a pool; and the **Terramar course** at Sitges (www.golfterramar. com). For additional information, visit www.catgolf.com.

SAILING AND WATERSPORTS

For sailing information, you can contact the **Reial Club Marítim** (www.maritimbarcelona.org). For watersports and equipment hire in general, try **Base Nautica de la Mar Bella** on Platja Mar Bella, Av. Litoral (www.basenautica.org).

SKIING

Skiing in the Pyrenees is popular. Most resorts are within two hours of Barcelona; some are accessible by train, and there are cheap

Inhabitant of the Parc Zoológic

> ## NOTES
>
> Barcelona's biggest and best flea market is Els Encants, which pulsates with action every Monday, Wednesday, Friday and Saturday 9am–7/8pm near Plaça de les Glòries Catalanes (Glòries metro). Some of the stuff is good, some is rubbish, but it's all good fun. For stamps, coins and memorabilia, hotfoot it to the Plaça Reial on Sunday morning, or venture to the Sant Antoni market for records and books. Plaça Sant Josep Oriol has a weekend art fair, and there is an antiques fair every Thursday (in summer) in the cathedral square.

weekend excursions available. Information can be obtained from the **Asociació Catalana d'Estacions d'Esquí** (www.catneu.tg1.com).

SHOPPING

While for sheer size and scope Barcelona cannot compete with Paris or other fashion capitals, it is one of the world's most stylish cities – architecture, fashion and decoration are thoroughly permeated by Catalan *disseny* (design). All of this makes for great shopping, whether you're looking for unique clothing by a hot local designer or something chic for the home. Traditional arts and crafts have a place here too, from basketwork to ceramics, and many artists and craftworkers have workshops that are open to the public. Catalonia still thrives on family-owned shops, and window shopping on the Rambla de Catalunya or Passeig de Gràcia is a delight.

WHERE TO SHOP

Passeig de Gràcia, Rambla de Catalunya and Diagonal are great for **clothing**, jewellery and design stores and art galleries. Alternative fashion shops, galleries and street markets are dotted around the Barri Gòtic, El Born and El Raval. Plaça de Catalunya is the jumping-off point for some of the best shopping streets: Portal de l'Àngel, Pelai and Carrer Portaferrisa are always swarming. The upper section of La Rambla has some leading clothing stores, though tacky souvenir shops are rife.

Some of the best spots for **antiques** are in the Old Town, along Banys Nous, Carrer de la Palla and Baixada Santa Eulàlia, between the cathedral and the Plaça del Pi. An antiques market is held every Thursday in the cathedral square. There is a scattering of individual shops around the Eixample, and Bulevar dels Antiquaris, at Passeig de Gràcia 57, conceals a maze of dealers.

For **art**, explore Consell de Cent, in the Eixample; the Born, a hot gallery-browsing area; and the streets around contemporary art museum MACBA in El Raval. There is a string of galleries on Petritxol, near Plaça del Pi, and Montcada, clustered around the Museu Picasso.

Ceramics, from traditional tiles, plates and bowls with brightly coloured glazing, to more modern creations, can be found in the streets around the cathedral and along Montcada. Quality ceramics and handicrafts are sold at Art Escudellers (Escudellers 23–25). Many museum shops also sell high-end art and design items.

Stalls at the Els Encants flea market on Plaça de les Glòries

For quintessential Catalan and international **interiors**, Passage Barcelona (Abat Samsó 7), Barcelona's trendy design emporium, is full of funky furniture, unconventional art and timeless fashion – a great place to be inspired.

Colmado Quílez (Rambla de Catalunya 63, https://lafuente.es) is a classic Catalan **grocery**, with packaged goods, fine wines, cheeses and imported beer in a photogenic corner shop. Since 1851, the place to find roasted nuts, dried fruits, coffee and spices has been Casa Gispert (Sombrerers 23, www.casagispert.com) near Santa Maria del Mar. For a religious experience and a history lesson with your shopping, visit Caelum (Carrer de la Palla 8, www.caelumbarcelona.com), which stocks a variety of products produced by Trappist monks, such as beers, honey, candles and cheese plus a delicious assortment of tea and pastries. Downstairs is a cellar tearoom where the ancient foundations of fourteenth-century women's baths were uncovered and are open to the public.

La Boqueria – the best place for fresh produce

The ultimate food shopping experience in Barcelona, of course, is Mercat La Boqueria (www.boqueria.info; see page 35) for fish, meat, fruit, vegetables, charcuterie and olives. It's open Monday to Saturday till 8pm and it's not to be missed.

WHAT TO BUY

For cutting-edge **clothing** by the late Catalonian designer Antonio Miró, check out his eponymous signature store at Calle Enric Granados 46. The dynamic Custo Barcelona has stores in a string of locations across town, including La Rambla 109. **Espadrilles** are a popular casual summer footwear in Spain whose defining characteristic is its soles made of esparto rope. Head straight to the closest La Manual for the best quality and widest selection.

A popular souvenir, the **porrón** is a Catalan wine pitcher with a thin spout, designed for pouring *vino* in a stream directly into your mouth. Head to the nearest El Corte Inglés for the best selection.

The Catalan region is famous for producing some of the highest-quality **olive oil** in the world, and a large variety can be found in shops throughout Barcelona. Visit markets such as Mercat de Sant Antoni (Carrer del Comte d'Urgell 1) for the finest olive oil at affordable prices. You will see **turrón** for sale in sweet shops all over Barcelona – a type of nougat that is a favourite with locals. Try La Campana (Carrer Princesa 36 & 16), a specialist confectionary shop that's been churning out the stuff since 1890.

Get saucy and pick up a bottle of *romesco*, *all i oli* or *xató*. **Romesco**, a zippy blend of roasted red pepper, tomato and almond, is often served with *calçots* (grilled green onion) and other roasted vegetables, while **xató** (a thicker version of *romesco*) is doused on salads and the Catalan dish *xatonada* (salted cod, tuna, anchovies, olives and escarole). La Boqueria market is the place to go to buy traditional sauces. If you want to make *all i oli* or other sauces yourself, buy a Spanish-style **morteros** (mortar and pestle); they are yellow with bright green splatters and are extremely practical.

Home to one of the world's greatest football clubs, it will come as no surprise that *barceloneses* are totally obsessed with the game. Pick up **football memorabilia** at the stadium gift shop or risk the plentiful souvenir stores for affordable (but probably fake) football-themed gifts.

BARCELONA FOR CHILDREN

Most of the major museums and galleries run children's activity programmes, especially in school holidays. These range from art and craft workshops at the **Fundació Joan Miró** and MACBA to chocolate-making at the **Museu de la Xocolata** (Carrer del Comerç 36). Museums with a special interest for children include **Museu Blau** (Plaza Leonardo Da Vinci 4–5), **CosmoCaixa** science museum (Carrer d'Isaac Newton 26) and **Museu de Cera** wax museum (Passatge de la Banca 7).

There are often children's puppet shows, music, mime and clowns at the Fundació Joan Miró, usually at weekends and holidays. **Jove Teatre Regina** (C/Sèneca 22, Gràcia, www.jtregina. com) puts on music and comedy productions for kids, though these are usually in Catalan. Children's activities are also held at the Pati Llimona on C/Regomir near the Town Hall (Ajuntament) in Pl. Sant Jaume (www.patillimona.net).

The CosmoCaixa science museum

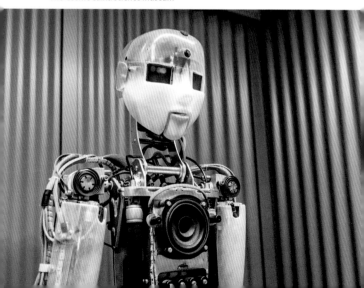

Always a hit with kids, the **zoo** (Ciutadella Park, www.zoo barcelona.cat) has enclosures filled with lions, tigers and bears along with numerous other species, while Ciutadella Park itself, with boats for hire, is fun and shady.

The **Poble Espanyol** (Montjuïc, www.poble-espanyol.com), a recreation of a Spanish village, is popular with families, both locals and visitors, and manages to interest teenagers as well as children. Elsewhere, **Tibidabo amusement park** (Parc d'Atraccions, www.tibidabo.cat) is good fun for all ages, and kids love to arrive there on the Tramvia Blau (see page 82).

CALENDAR OF EVENTS

February (second week) Feast of Santa Eulàlia, a winter *Festa Major* that's a low-key version of La Mercè (see 24 September).

February–March Carnival, preceding Lent, is a wild celebration. Sitges carnival is the best in the region.

Setmana Santa/Easter Palm Sunday processions and services on Holy Thursday/Good Friday.

23 April Feast of Sant Jordi (St George). Stalls piled with books and roses are set up in La Rambla and Passeig de Gràcia.

27 April Feast of Virgin of Montserrat. Liturgical rituals, choir singing and sardana dancing.

11 May Sant Ponç. Herb fair in Carrer de l'Hospital.

Mid-June Corpus Christi. Carpets of flowers and processions in Sitges. In Barcelona 'dancing eggs' are balanced on the spray of the cathedral fountain and fountains in other courtyards in the Barri Gòtic.

Mid- to late June Barcelona's high-octane festival of art, design and dance music attracts thousands of revellers to Sonar.

23–24 June Sant Joan (St John). A major event in Catalonia, with fireworks, feasting and flowing cava.

July Grec Summer Festival of theatre, dance, classical, pop and rock music.

Flag waving on the National Day of Catalonia

15–21 August Festa Major de Gràcia. Street parties, parades, fireworks and concerts in Gràcia neighbourhood.

11 September Diada. National Day of Catalonia, with demonstrations and flag waving.

24 September La Mercè. Barcelona's week-long festival in honour of its patron, Mare del Déu de la Mercè (Our Lady of Mercy). Fireworks, music and dancing in the streets. Head to Plaça St Jaume to see *castells*; the Ball de Gegants is a parade of huge papier-mâché figures; Correfoc is a rowdy nocturnal parade of devils and fire-spitting dragons, not to be missed.

1–23 December Santa Llùcia Fair. A market selling Nativity figurines, art, crafts and Christmas trees in front of the cathedral.

26 December Sant Esteve (St Stephen's Day). Families meet for an even larger meal than that eaten on Christmas Day.

Food and drink

Barcelona's food scene has changed immeasurably in the past few years, with a raft of new restaurants and craft brewpubs and a rise in popularity (and return) of food markets that have always been central to Catalan cooking.

The city offers an attractive mix of haute cuisine, and the classic rustic cooking that has fed Catalans for centuries. These traditions are being reimagined by a new breed of restaurateurs. The man behind this renaissance is Catalan chef Ferran Adrià, whose triple-Michelin-starred *El Bulli* on the Costa Brava helped put contemporary Spanish cuisine on the map. Now a cookery foundation, the kitchen has spawned a generation of regional chefs working in the city's finest restaurants.

Talent like Jordi Vilà, Carles Abellán, Ramón Freixa and the trio behind *Disfrutar*, which topped the World's 50 Best Restaurants 2024 list, are pushing the boundaries of Spanish cuisine with

WHERE TO EAT IN BARCELONA

Barcelona's restaurants begin with a major advantage: superb ingredients, as anyone who has entered one of the city's great covered markets can attest. The gorgeous terracotta and steel-roofed Mercat de Sant Antoni reopened in 2019, whilst the happily chaotic La Boqueria market continues to be a kaleidoscopic thrill for the senses. You can also eat cheaply in *cafeterías*, where you will usually be offered a *plat combinat* (*plato combinado* in Castilian Spanish), usually meat or fish with chips and salad, served on the same plate. Not the best way to eat, but fast and inexpensive. Your choices are not limited to restaurants and *cafeterías*. Most bars (also called *tabernas*, *bodegas* and *cervecerías*) serve food, often of a high standard. Here you can have a selection of tapas, sandwiches (*bocadillos* in Spanish, *bocats* or *entrepans* in Catalan) or *limited plats combinats* at almost any time of the day.

theatrical and daringly modern takes, inspired by the culinary traditions of Catalonia.

Alongside this revolution, a rash of international restaurants, from taquerias to world-class sushi joints, are springing up around the Old Town and Eixample, El Born and the uptown residential neighbourhoods of *Barrios Altos*. The boom in craft beer hasn't escaped Barcelona either. The city boasts its own modest 'craft beer mile' with *Garage Beer Co* brewpub (C/Consell de Cent 261, www. garagebeer.co) being an early fixture on the scene.

TOP TEN THINGS TO TRY

Catalan cooking is based on *cuina del mercat* – market cuisine. Fresh fish and seafood dominate the menu, and fruits and vegetables are at their freshest. Mountain-cured hams and spicy sausages, spit-roasted meats and fowl with aromatic herbs are specialities. Expect *all i oli* (garlic and olive oil mayonnaise), seasonal produce from the countryside, and wild mushrooms – *bolets*. The foundation of rustic Catalan cuisine is *pa amb tomàquet* – slices of rustic bread rubbed with garlic and fresh tomatoes, doused

---

WHEN TO EAT

Barceloneses, like all Spaniards, eat late. Lunch usually isn't eaten until 2 or 3pm. Dinner is served from about 9pm until 11.30pm, although at weekends people sometimes don't sit down to eat until midnight. You could always adopt the Spanish system, which is to pace yourself for the late hours by eating tapas. Typically, breakfast is a simple affair, a coffee and a pastry to tide you over until lunch. Nearly all restaurants offer a lunchtime *menú del día*, a daily set menu that is a bargain. For a fixed price you'll receive three courses: a starter – often soup or salad – a main dish and dessert. Typically, the cost is about half what you'd expect to pay if you ordered from the regular menu. Reservations are recommended at Barcelona's more popular restaurants. Many are closed on Sunday night.

Freshly prepared tapas

with olive oil and sprinkled with coarse salt. Here are the must-try dishes you'll want to experience while in Barcelona.

1. PAELLA

Originating in Valencia, paella is a classic Spanish rice dish that is traditionally meant to be shared: cooked in a large shallow pan over an open fire and then placed on the table for all to dig into. The most common types are *paella valenciana* (made with chicken and rabbit) and *paella de mariscos* (seafood), which are both typically made with a mix of saffron, paprika, garlic, tomatoes and olive oil. The dish is normally served with a side of green beans, and sometimes a salad. If you want to sample the best paella, bypass tourist-trap restaurants, especially on La Rambla, in favour of backstreet neighbourhood haunts in districts like Sant Pere, La Ribera, El Raval and Poble Sec.

2. TAPAS

The small plates for which Spanish bars are world-famous come in dozens of tempting varieties, from olives and salted almonds, to baby squid, fried green *pimientos* (peppers), garlicky shrimp, lobster mayonnaise, meatballs, *patatas bravas*, wedges of omelette, Catalan sausage and local cheeses. The list is almost endless, and can be surprisingly creative, especially at the now extremely popular Basque tapas joints. A dish larger than a tapa is a *porción*. A large serving, meant to be shared, is a *ración*, and half of this, a media *ración*. Best of all, tapas are usually available throughout the day, and are a great way to try new flavours. Find a tapas bar with a fast-moving line, as it usually means the food is fresh and it's a sign of quality and authenticity.

An evening at Mercat de la Boqueria

3. ESCALIVADA

This simple, delicious side dish of smoky grilled vegetables originated in Catalonia, and typically consists of roasted eggplant and bell peppers with olive oil and often onion, tomato, minced garlic and salt. Its name refers to the unique cooking process: *escalivada* comes from the Catalan word *escalibar,* which means to roast over the embers of a wood fire – the dish is allowed to cool before eating, as the flavours are more pronounced at room temperature. It pairs well with fish and grilled meats, or can be enjoyed alone with crisp toast.

4. BOCADILLO DE CALAMARES

A traditional Spanish sandwich of a baguette-type of bread filled with fried squid and garnished with lemon, parsley or other herbs. It is typically served with a side of *all i oli*, a traditional Catalan sauce made of garlic, olive oil and lemon juice. It's a popular street food and can be found all over Barcelona at tapas bars and seafood joints.

5. BOMBAS

A staple on the Catalonian tapas menu, *bombas* are crispy mashed potato balls spiked with spices and mixed with meat and vegetables. Each restaurant holds its own recipe close to its chest and claims to have the best in town.

Bocadillo de calamares, a traditional Spanish sandwich packed with fried squid, with a side of all i oli

Crema catalana

6. ESCUDELLA

Chefs across the region have their own interpretations of *escudella*, a Catalan soup-like stew made with seasonal vegetables, meats and local sausages. Noodles are often added along with heavily spiced and characteristically large meatballs. It is favoured in the winter months for its comforting warmth. Expect a generous serving in restaurants, though you might have to wait for it.

7. PATATAS BRAVAS

Spanish *patatas bravas*, or *papas bravas*, meaning 'spicy potatoes', are hand-cut fried potatoes slathered in a punchy red sauce. Another classic at Barcelona's tapas bars, it's the sauce that gives the dish its rich, smoky flavour and distinguishes it from other fried potato recipes.

8. JAMÓN IBÉRICO

It is primarily Black Iberian pigs that produce *jamón ibérico*, the king of Spanish hams. The curing process involves salting the meat for around ten to fourteen days, and then the pork leg is dry-hung for around ninety days, where it develops the natural mould that coats and protects the ham. Tuck into paper-thin slices at any of the more upmarket tapas bars around town – and dig deep into your wallet to pay for the privilege.

9. TURRÓN

The Spanish have a sweet tooth and particularly love *turrón* (*torró* in Catalan/Valenciano), a nougat candy with almonds and honey. Sink your teeth into either the crunchy (often called Alicante) or the soft (Jijona), which has a smooth consistency almost like peanut butter, and decide which you prefer. The two leading brands are Lobo and 1880, though you'll find many others throughout Barcelona, including small-batch boutique producers.

10. DESSERTS

When it comes to dessert, *flan* is ubiquitous, but there's a homemade version, the *crema catalana* (egg custard topped with caramelised sugar). Other popular treats include *mel i mato* (soft white cheese covered in honey), *pastisset* (almond cakes), *carquinyolis* (a rusk-like biscuit) or *catanies* (chocolate studded with Marcona almonds). The finest sweet delicacies can be found in local pastry shops.

DRINKS

Wine is a constant at the Catalan table. In addition to an assortment of fine wines from across Spain, Barcelona presents an opportunity to try some excellent regional wines. Penedès, the grape-growing region just outside Barcelona, produces some excellent wines, including *cava*, Spain's sparkling wine. *Cava* goes

Dry Martini cocktail bar

well with seafood and most tapas. Among Penedès reds, the best ones to try include Torres Gran Coronas, Raimat and Jean León. Wines from the Priorat area are superb, robust, expensive reds that rival the best in Spain. Don't be surprised to be offered red wine chilled in hot weather. White wines from the La Rueda region are generally good.

Sangría is a favourite, made of wine and fruit fortified with brandy, but it's drunk more by visitors than locals. Spanish beers, available in bottles and on draft, are generally light and refreshing. A glass of draught beer is a *caña*.

You'll find every kind of sherry (*jerez*) here. The pale, dry *fino* is sometimes drunk not only as an apéritif but also with soup and fish courses. Rich dark *oloroso* goes well after dinner. Spanish brandy varies from excellent to rough: you usually get what you pay for. Other spirits are made under licence in Spain, and are usually pretty cheap. Imported Scotch whisky is fashionable, but expensive. It is advisable to request a particular brand when asking for spirits.

Coffee is served black (*solo/sol*), with a spot of milk (*cortado/tallat*), or half and half with hot milk (*con leche/amb llet*). *Horchata de chufa*, made with ground tiger nuts, is popular in summer, and is sold in bars called *horchaterías* which also sell ice cream.

TO HELP YOU ORDER

Could we have a table, please? **¿Nos puede dar una mesa, por favor?**

Do you have a set menu? **¿Tiene un menú del día?**

I'd like a/an/some… **Quisiera…**

The bill, please **La cuenta, por favor**

MENU READER

a la plancha grilled

agua water

al ajillo in garlic

arroz rice

asado roasted

atún tuna

azúcar sugar

bacalao dried salt cod

bocadillo sandwich

calamares squid

cangrejo crab

caracoles snails

la carne de cerdo pork

la carne de vaca beef

cerveza beer

champiñones mushrooms

chorizo spicy sausage

chuletón T-bone steak

cordero lamb

croquetas croquettes

ensalada salad

filete steak

flan caramel custard

gambas prawns

gazpacho cold tomato soup

helado ice cream

huevo egg

jamón serrano cured ham

judías beans

langosta lobster

leche milk

lomo pork loin

marisco shellfish

mejillones mussels

morcilla black pudding

pan bread

patata potato

patatas fritas chips

pescado fish

picante spicy

pollo chicken

pulpo octopus

queso cheese

salchicha sausage

salsa sauce

ternera veal

tortilla omelette

trucha trout

verduras vegetables

vino wine

Places to eat

Each restaurant and café reviewed in this Guide is accompanied by a price category, based on the cost of a three-course meal (or similar) for one, with house wine:

€€€€ = over €60
€€€ = €40–60
€€ = €25–40
€ = below €25

CIUTAT VELLA (OLD TOWN)

Agut Carrer Gignàs 16, tel: 93-315 1709. This small 1924-founded restaurant is hidden away on a small street in the Barri Gòtic behind Passeig de Colom. Relaxed and homely, the menu is packed with plenty of Catalan flavour and lots of daily specials, which might include home-made cannelloni, fish or game. The excellent and huge rice dishes are meant to be shared. €€

Biocenter Carrer del Pintor Fortuny 25, www.restaurantebiocenter.es. Vegetarian restaurant serving huge portions in a friendly atmosphere. Located just off La Rambla, north of La Boqueria market. €

El Bosc de Les Fades Passatge de la Banca 7, www.boscdelesfades.com. This dark and moody restaurant – a surreal fairy-tale escape from the world outside – is filled with lantern-strung trees, fairies and waterfalls. Tapas are served but it's the drinks and quirky surroundings that draw people in. €€

Caelum Carrer de la Palla 8, www.caelumbarcelona.com. The lovingly packaged confections in this upscale café-pâtisserie (the name is Latin for 'heaven') are made in convents and monasteries across Spain. Choose from *frutas de almendra* (marzipan sweeties) from Seville, Benedictine preserves or Cistercian cookies – or hunker down for cakes and coffee in the atmospheric basement crypt. **€**

Can Culleretes Carrer d'en Quintana 5, www.culleretes.com. Barcelona's oldest restaurant has served traditional Catalan food since 1786. It is cosy and informal, and serves classic dishes like *espinacs à la catalana* (spinach with pine nuts and raisins) and *botifarra* (spicy country sausage). Fixed-price menus are available weekdays. Near La Rambla but feels like a different world. **€€**

Los Caracoles Carrer d'Escudellers 14, www.loscaracoles.es. 'The Snails' is famous for its chicken roasting on a spit outside, on one of the Old Quarter's busiest pedestrian streets, just south of Plaça Reial. It has been around since 1835, and while it's touristy it is fun, and you can dine on a fine meal of fish, game, roasted chicken or lamb, in addition, of course, to snails. **€€€**

La Dolça Herminia **€** Carrer de les Magdalenes 27, www.grupandilana. com. Close to Via Laietana, this smart but very reasonably priced haunt has an imaginative menu. No reservations. **€€**

Fonda España Carrer de Sant Pau 9, www.hotelespanya.com. A smart restaurant sheltered within the *Hotel España*, the dining room was designed by *modernista* architect Domènech i Montaner, while the back room is adorned with murals by Ramón Casas, a contemporary of Picasso. Renowned Michelin-starred chef Martín Berasategui brings experimental culinary endeavours to patrons – and at reasonable prices. Next to the Teatre del Liceu. **€€€**

El Gran Café Carrer d'Avinyó 9, http://restaurantelgrancafe.com. Looks like an English pub on the outside, but has a handsome *modernista* interior, and is well-known for its Catalan cuisine. The set menu is very good value, otherwise it is rather expensive. **€€€**

Els Quatre Gats (4 Gats) Carrer de Montsió 3, www.4gats.com. 'The Four Cats', which was once the hangout of Picasso and pals, serves simple Catalan fare in fabulous *modernista* surroundings. The *menú del día* (lunch only) is a good deal, but really the atmosphere's the main calling card. €€

El Quim de la Boqueria La Boqueria, La Rambla, www.elquimdela boqueria.com. This is one of several stalls in La Boqueria market where it's a treat to pull up a stool and see the freshest produce grilled before your eyes. Don't be surprised to see locals eating a hearty breakfast of pigs' trotters washed down with a glass of red wine. €€

Rasoterra Carrer del Palau 5, www.rasoterra.cat. A plant-based diet doesn't have to be boring, and this lovely bistro has some ingenious recipes to prove it. The vegan and vegetarian options include glazed white asparagus with miso, figs and walnuts and orecchiette with creamy courgette and pepper sauce. *Rasoterra* supports the Slow Food movement, so if you're looking for a place to chill while enjoying some exciting and new tastes – this is where you need to go. €€

Rodrigo Carrer de l'Argenteria 67, tel: 93-310 3020. An authentic family-run local bar, not far from the church of Santa Maria del Mar, serving delicious set menus at a good price. Don't miss its pre-lunch *vermut*, an intoxicating house speciality. €

Senyor Parellada Carrer de l'Argenteria 37, www.senyorparellada.com. An attractive, popular restaurant in La Ribera, close to the church of Santa Maria del Mar. Both the surroundings and the creative Catalan menu are sophisticated but unpretentious. €€€

Sesamo Carrer de Sant Antoni Abat 52, tel: 93-441 6411. A bit off the beaten track, close to Sant Antoni market on the western edge of El Raval, this inviting vegetarian joint is worth a visit for its fantastic range of dishes and an excellent tapas tasting menu. €

Shunka Carrer del Sagristans 5, www.koyshunka.com. Try the freshest of sushi and sashimi and much more at this excellent Japanese restaurant hidden behind the cathedral. It's all prepared before your eyes, and there's a fun, buzzy atmosphere. €€€

TAPAS BARS

Bar Lobo Carrer del Pintor Fortuny 3, www.grupotragaluz.com/restaurantes/bar-lobo. The hippest member of the Tragaluz empire attracts a cool crowd with its stylish interior, lounging terrace in a busy pedestrian street, and combination of light Mediterranean and Japanese dishes. Open late for drinks at weekends. €€

Cal Pep Pl. de les Olles 8, La Ribera, https://calpep.com. There's no equal in town for sea-to-plate and market-fresh tapas. You will have to queue (no reservations allowed), and prices are high for what's effectively a bar meal (up to €50 a head), but it's worth it for the likes of impeccably fried shrimp, grilled sea bass, Catalan sausage and beans, and baby squid and chickpeas. There's also a small, intimate dining room and a handful of tables outside. €€€

Euskal Etxea Placeta de Montcada 1–3, www.euskaletxeataberna.com. A great Basque tapas bar with a huge choice that has quickly established itself as a firm local favourite. Excellent meals, served in the restaurant area, are more expensive. Located at the bottom of Carrer de Montcada, south of the Museu Picasso. €€

Irati Taverna Basca Carrer del Cardenal Casañas 17, www.iratitaverna basca.com. In the same group as Euskal Etxea, this immensely popular Basque tapas joint, just off La Rambla at the edge of the Barri Gòtic, is always packed. At lunchtime and in early evening, heaving trays of tapas (*pintxos* in Basque) are laid out on the bar. It's a bit like a party, except that you have to keep track of the number of small plates and glasses of wine you've had, and the cheerful attendants tally it all up before you leave. Full menu also available. €€

Mesón del Café Carrer de la Llibreteria 16, tel: 93-315 0754. An iconic locals' café, opened in 1909 and still full of atmosphere. Great for quick coffees, and perhaps a tapa or two. It's tiny and you'll probably have to stand, though there is a dinky nook at the back with a few tables. €€

La Vinya del Senyor Plaça Santa Maria 5. Delightful wine bar with a large terrace overlooking the facade of Santa Maria del Mar, in the Born. Offers interesting wines and *cava* by the glass, and a few select tapas to absorb the booze. €

El Xampanyet Carrer de Montcada 22, www.elxampanyet.es. Situated near the Museu Picasso and El Born, this *azulejo*-tiled bar specialises in *cava* and some of the best tapas in town, especially the Cantabrian anchovies. An old-school classic. €

EIXAMPLE

La Bodegueta Rambla de Catalunya 100, https://labodeguetarambla. com. It's easy to pass by this simple *bodega,* on the corner of La Rambla and Carrer de Provença, without even noticing it. Regulars pop in at any hour for *jamón serrano* (cured ham) and a glass of rioja. Good wine selection. No credit cards. €

Cinc Sentits Carrer d'Entença 60, www.cincsentits.com. An ideal choice for foodies: Michelin-starred chef Jordi Artal's tasting menu is a guaranteed gourmet experience and a good example of new Catalan cuisine. It's at the intersection of the streets d'Aribau and d'Aragó. €€€€

Disfrutar Carrer de Villaroel 163, www.disfrutarbarcelona.com. The hottest restaurant in Barcelona belongs to three former head chefs of the now-closed *El Bulli*, for many years considered the best in the world. The creativity here is off the charts. Tasting menus (€175) are an endless procession of tiny delights that will make you groan with pleasure – at least until the bill arrives. €€€€

Lasarte Carrer de Mallorca 259, https://restaurantlasarte.com. Quite simply one of the best restaurants in Spain, with three Michelin stars to prove it. Basque gastronomic superstar Martín Berasategui has his name on the door but it's Paolo Casagrande who runs the kitchen, turning out a creative tasting menu that's strong on perfectionism and clean flavours. Send a message of apology to your bank manager before you reach for the wine list. €€€€

Maison Coffee Carrer de Provença 158, tel: 93-451 1309. Like something out of a Scandi design lookbook, this sleek coffeeshop serves third-wave coffee and Instagrammable lattes. The home-made cakes and pastries are excellent, and just as picturesque. €

Moments Hotel Mandarin Oriental, Passeig de Gràcia 38–40, www. mandarinoriental.com. Michelin starred *Moments* is certainly impressive and proving a popular fine-dining venue. Helmed by Raül Balam, son of famous chef Carme Ruscalleda, the menu sees a return to traditional Catalan roots. €€€€

Piscolabis Rambla de Catalunya 27, www.piscolabisrestaurant.es. Very good value for money, and an excellent choice of tapas to sample and share. The warm and friendly service will make you feel right at home. Outside seating is available if you'd rather sit in the sun than the well-designed interior. €€

Roast Club Café Carrer de València, 143, www.roastclub.coffee. Some of the finest coffee in the city can be found here. It also serves decent sandwiches, salads and cakes. €€

Taktika Berri Carrer de València 169, www.taktikaberri.net. Basque restaurants are popping up across Barcelona. One of the best in town is this family-owned and -operated tapas bar and restaurant in a converted textile workshop, close to the intersection of streets València and Muntaner. The *pintxos* (tapas) are excellent, as are the creative starters and desserts. €€€

Tapas 24 Carrer de la Diputació 269, www.carlesabellan.com. At this trendy bar, not far from Girona metro, you can taste classic tapas by a new generation of Catalan star chefs. You might have to queue, but it's worth it and the bustling atmosphere is absorbing. €€

Tragaluz Passatge de la Concepció 5, www.grupotragaluz.com. Barcelona's love affair with food comes to life in this trendy, colourful restaurant tucked away down a tiny passageway off Passeig de Gràcia. After a complete overhaul, *Tragaluz* ('Skylight') allows you to dine beneath the stars thanks to a huge glass roof, and has a new, fresh approach. The Mediterranean cuisine still hits the mark but with a lighter touch. Alternatively, you can dine on oysters, sushi or Japanese grilled food at the bar downstairs. €€€€

WATERFRONT/PORT OLÍMPIC

Agua Passeig Marítim 30, www.grupotragaluz.com. Almost on the beach, with indoor and outdoor tables, the modern and attractive *Agua* gets very busy, so booking is essential, especially if you want to nab a table on the terrace. Expect well-executed fish, rice dishes and imaginative vegetarian plates. €€€

Can Ganassa Plaça de la Barceloneta 6, www.restaurantcanganassa. es. This popular seafood haunt on the main square in Barceloneta serves up excellent fish dishes using that day's catch, as well as a wide array of delicious tapas and sandwiches. €€

Can Majó Carrer de l'Almirante Aixada 23, www.canmajo.es. It's difficult to find an authentic paella in the touristed centre, but at this Barceloneta classic you can't go wrong. A handful of pleasant dining rooms and a sea-facing terrace. €€€

La Cova Fumada Carrer del Baluard 56, Barceloneta, tel: 93-221 4061. Behind an unassuming brown wooden door on Barceloneta's market square (there's no sign) you'll find this rough-and-ready tavern with battered marble tables and antique barrels. It might not look like much but the food's great, made using in-season ingredients straight from the market, from griddled prawns to fried artichokes. €€

La Flor del Norte Passeig de Colom 10, tel: 93-315 2659. An excellent choice for a low-cost meal, *La Flor del Norte* turns out faithful renditions of classic tapas and seafood dishes at more-than-reasonable prices. The sizzling clay pots of paella are as good as you're going to get around here, and at under €20 for two portions, no less. Book ahead: the terrace swells quickly, and indoors the strip lighting dampens the atmosphere; nonetheless, the price and location are unbeatable. €

Marina Coastal Club Carrer de la Marina 1, www.hotelartsbarcelona. com. Superb seafood served in an unforgettable setting: on the rooftop of *Hotel Arts*, right next to the poolside. The dishes look like *modernist* art creations, and the staff know their stuff about Spanish wine. The menu isn't cheap – best for a light lunch or lavish blowout. €€€

Restaurant 7 Portes Passeig d'Isabel II 14, www.7portes.com. Not far from the *Cap de Barcelona* artwork, this is one of Barcelona's most venerable institutions, now sympathetically restored, and a favourite for special occasions since 1836. *Restaurant 7 Portes* ('Seven Doors') is famous for its rice classics; favourites include black rice with squid ink and an assortment of paellas. Portions are huge, the dining rooms elegant and the waiters old-style attentive. €€€

Xiringuíto Escribà Avinguda Litoral Mar 62, Platja Bogatell, www. restaurantsescriba.com/xiringuitoescriba/en. Lots of imaginative fish and rice plates in this down-to-earth, family-run spot, right by the beach, east of Port Olímpic. And, yes, they are the same Escribà family that are renowned for their chocolates and pastries, so the puddings are guaranteed to be marvellous. €€€

Xiroi Ca la Nuri Passeig Marítim de la Nova Icària 38, www.xiroi.calanuri. com. A dependable seafood restaurant known for its rice dishes, tapas and fish mains. This location has been serving the local Catalan community since 1950. €€€

GRÀCIA AND ABOVE THE DIAGONAL

Bilbao Carrer del Perill 33, www.restaurantbilbao.com. Best at lunchtime when the local crowd are there, this bustling restaurant has heaps of atmosphere and uses the freshest market produce. It's across the Avinguda Diagonal northwest of Diagonal metro, off Carrer de Corsega. €€€

Botafumeiro Carrer Gran de Gràcia 81, www.botafumeiro.es. Barcelona's top seafood restaurant and reputedly the King of Spain's favourite. It's large and informal, with lots of action. Much of the fresh seafood is flown in daily from the owner's home territory, Galicia. You can feast on great shellfish and seafood tapas here (which keeps costs down). To score a seat at the seafood bar, visit off-hours, earlier than local people would eat. Just above the Diagonal, at the beginning of the Gràcia neighbourhood. €€€€

Travel essentials

PRACTICAL INFORMATION

ACCESSIBLE TRAVEL

Barcelona has plenty of accessible hotels; visit www.barcelona-access.cat for details or check with the tourist office. Many museums and historic buildings are wheelchair-friendly. The beaches have suitable access, and there are many adapted public toilets. Some bus and metro lines have facilities for disabled travellers (see www.tmb.cat).

ACCOMMODATION

Hotels of greatest interest to visitors are those in Eixample or the Ciutat Vella (Old Town), which includes La Rambla, Barri Gòtic and El Born. The Old Town provides the best choice, though visitors who stay on or near La Rambla will have to endure late-night noise and crowds.

Many old buildings have been converted into tourist apartments, with better deals away from the centre. The most recent additions are along the waterfront and Diagonal Mar, where you can expect a high standard for a reasonable price, with speedy access to the beach.

I'd like a double/single room **Quisiera una habitación doble/sencilla**
with/without bath/shower **con/sin baño/ducha**
double bed **cama matrimonial**
What's the rate per night? **¿Cuál es el precio por noche?**
Is breakfast included? **¿Está incluído el desayuno?**

AIRPORTS

Barcelona's international airport, El Prat de Llobregat (www.aena.es) is twelve kilometres (seven miles) south of the city. You can reach the city centre by train, bus, metro or taxi, or rent a car. The national train service, RENFE (www.renfe.com), runs trains from the airport every half-hour, stopping at Barcelona Sants and Passeig de Gràcia, taking about thirty minutes. The fare is €5.15, though it is worth buying a T10 card (see page 139). The metro line L9 stops at both terminals and connects with three urban metro lines (L1, L3, L5). Note that a special ticket (€4.50) is needed to ride the airport line. Aerobuses (www.aerobusbarcelona.es) depart every 5–10min from each terminal for Pl. Catalunya, daily 5.35am–1am, calling at several points en route. There is also a public bus (No. 46) linking the airport terminals with Pl. Espanya in the city centre. Taxis charge about €30 to the city centre. Agree a fare before you start. They can charge extra for luggage.

APPS

Uber, Bolt and FREENOW are reliable taxi apps, often with options for eco-friendly vehicles. For navigating public transport, SMOU (www.smou.cat) is useful for real-time information on bus and metro services. Google Maps is great for finding your way around the city, while Citymapper (https://citymapper.com) offers step-by-step directions for navigating public transport. TheFork (www.thefork.co.uk) is an easy way to book a table at your choice restaurant online.

BICYCLE RENTAL

Cycles can be rented at several outlets, such as Budget Bikes on Calle Estruc 38 (www.budgetbikes.eu), or Green Bikes on Carrer Escudellers 48 (www.greenbikesbarcelona.com); both offer tours.

BUDGETING FOR YOUR TRIP

Barcelona has become much more expensive than it used to be and is on a par with other major European cities in many respects.

Transport to Barcelona. By budget airline or via Girona or Reus, travelling to Barcelona can be the cheapest part of your trip, from as little as €30 off-season, but obviously much more (€150–300 or over) on scheduled flights or from outside Europe. Buy in advance for the best deals.

Accommodation. Most hotels do not include breakfast or the 10 percent VAT in their prices. Youth hostel €15–45 per person in a dorm; €40–80 in a *pension*; €90–225 en-suite double room; €225–450 top-end hotel. Note that these prices are average ranges, some specifics places may be much more expensive.

Meals. The *menú del día*, a fixed-price midday meal, is excellent value (usually from €12 upward). Spanish wines are mainly reasonably priced, even in fine restaurants. For a three-course evening meal in a mid-range restaurant with house wine, you can bank on €30–50 per person.

Drinks. Mineral water €0.80–€3; coffee €1.50–€4; fresh orange juice €3–4; *caña* (small draught beer) €2–4; glass of wine €3–4; spirit with mixer €4–7 or higher in clubs.

Local transport. Public transport within the city – buses and the metro – is inexpensive (see page 138) and taxis are reasonably priced.

Attractions. Museums and attractions range from free to over €17. Most municipal museums are free from 3pm on Sundays. The Art Ticket (www.articketbcn.org) is good value at €38, as it allows entrance to six art centres. Purchase online, at one of the centres or at tourist offices.

CAR HIRE

Barcelona has considerable parking problems and general congestion, and a car is more trouble than it's worth. If you do wish to hire a car to explore further afield, however, major international and Spanish companies have offices at the airport and in the city centre. A value-added tax (IVA) of 21 percent is added to the total charge, but will have been included if you have pre-paid before arrival (lowest rates are normally found online). Shorter rentals usually cost more per day than longer ones; three days' rental for a medium-sized family car costs €85–250 (more in peak season). Fully comprehensive insurance is required and should be included in the price; confirm that this is the case. Most companies require you to pay by credit card, or use your card as a deposit/guarantee. You must be over 21 and have had a licence for at least six months. A national driver's licence will suffice for EU nationals; others need an international licence.

I'd like to rent a car **Quisiera alquilar un coche**
for tomorrow **para mañana**
for one day/a week **por un día/una semana**

Please include full risk insurance **Haga el favor de incluir el seguro a todo riesgo**

Fill it up, please **Lleno, por favor**

May I return it to the airport? **¿Puedo dejarlo al aeropuerto?**

CLIMATE

Barcelona's Mediterranean climate assures sunshine most of the year and makes freezing temperatures rare even in the depths of winter (December to February). Spring and autumn are the most agreeable seasons for visiting. Midsummer can be hot and humid; at times a thick smog hangs over the city. Average temperatures are given below.

	J	F	M	A	M	J	J	A	S	O	N	D
°F	49	51	54	59	64	72	75	75	71	63	56	51
°C	9	10	12	14	18	22	24	24	22	18	13	11

CRIME AND SAFETY

You should exercise caution and be on your guard against pickpockets and bag snatchers (be wary of people offering 'assistance'), especially on or near La Rambla, the old city (particularly El Raval) and other major tourist areas, such as La Sagrada Família and crowded spots such as markets. Take the same precautions as you would in any city. Photocopy personal documents and leave the originals in your hotel.

The blue-clad anti-crime squads are out in force on the Ramblas and principal thoroughfares. Should you be the victim of a crime, make a *denuncia* (report) at the nearest police station (*comisaría* – vital if you are going to make an insurance claim).

The main one can be found in the Old Town at Nou de la Rambla 76–78, or telephone the Mossos d'Esquadra on 091 or 112. You can also report theft at most city hotels.

I want to report a theft **Quiero denunciar un robo**
My handbag/wallet/passport has been stolen **Me han robado el bolso/la cartera/el pasaporte**
Help! Thief! **¡Socorro! ¡Ladrón!**

DRIVING

In the event of a problem, drivers need a passport, a valid driving licence, registration papers and Green Card international insurance.

Road conditions. Roads within Barcelona are very congested and the ring roads around the city can be confusing. Roads and highways outside Barcelona are excellent, though you'll have to pay a toll *(peaje/peatje)* on most motorways *(autopistas)*. To cross into France via the La Jonquera border (160km/100 miles) from Barcelona, take the AP7 or E15 motorway. For road information, tel: 900-123 505.

Rules and regulations. Your car should display a nationality sticker. Front and rear seatbelts, a spare set of bulbs, visibility vests and two warning triangles are compulsory. Most fines for traffic offences are payable on the spot. Speed limits are 120kmh (75mph) on motorways, 100kmh (62mph) on dual carriageways, 90kmh (56mph) on main roads, 50kmh (30mph), or as marked, in urban areas. Speed checks are regular. The roads are patrolled by the Mossos d'Esquadra. The permitted blood-alcohol level is low and penalties stiff.

Registration papers **Permiso de circulación**
Is this the right road for…? **Es ésta la carretera hacia…?**
Full tank, please. **Lléne el depósito, por favor.**
normal/super **normal/super**
Please check the oil/tyres/battery. **Por favor, controle el aceite/los neumáticos/la batería.**
Can I park here? **¿Se puede aparcar aquí?**
My car has broken down. **Mi coche se ha estropeado.**
There's been an accident. **Ha habido un accidente.**

(International) driving licence **Carnet de conducir (internacional)**
Car registration papers **Permiso de circulación**
Green card **Tarjeta verde**

Road signs. You may see the following written signs in Spanish:
Parking. Finding a place to park can be difficult in Barcelona. Look for 'blue zones' (denoted by a blue 'P'), which are metered areas, or underground parking garages (also marked with a big blue-and-white 'P'). Green zones are reserved for residents with permits.
Breakdowns and assistance. In emergencies, tel: **112**.

¡Alto! Stop!
Aparcamiento Parking
Autopista Motorway
Ceda el paso Give way (yield)
Cruce peligroso Dangerous crossroads
Curva peligrosa Dangerous bend
Despacio Slow
Peligro Danger
Prohibido adelantar No overtaking (passing)
Prohibido aparcar No parking

ELECTRICITY

The standard is 220 volts. Power sockets (outlets) take round, two-pin plugs, so you will need an international adapter plug.

EMBASSIES AND CONSULATES

All embassies are in Madrid, but most Western European countries have consulates in Barcelona. A few notable consulates are listed below:
Canada: Pl. de Catalunya 9, 1º, 2a, tel: 93-412 7236.

UK: Avda Diagonal 477, 13º, tel: 93-366 6200, www.gov.uk.

US: Passeig de la Reina Elisenda 23, tel: 93-280 2227, https://es.usembassy.gov.

EMERGENCIES (see also Police, and Crime and safety)

General emergencies: **112**

Mossos d'Esquadra (Autonomous Catalan Police): **091**

Municipal (city) police: **092**

Fire: **080**

Ambulance: **061**

Police! **¡Policia!**

Fire! **¡Fuego!**

Stop! **¡Para!/¡Deténagase!**

Help! **¡Socorro!**

Thief! **¡Ladrón!**

GETTING THERE

By air (see also Airports). Barcelona's airport is linked by regularly scheduled, daily non-stop flights from across Europe. Some services from the US and Canada are direct; others fly through Madrid (or in some cases, Lisbon). From Australia, Singapore and New Zealand, regular one-stop flights travel directly to Barcelona or Madrid. Flying times: London, about two hours; New York, approximately eight hours.

Iberia, the Spanish national airline, covers most countries in shared arrangements with their own carriers (www.iberia.com).

By sea. Balearia has a service to/from Ibiza, Mallorca and Menorca (tel: 902 160 180; www.balearia.com). Acciona-Trasmediterránea (Moll Sant Bertran 3, www.trasmediterranea.es) also operates ferries to the Balearic Islands. Grimaldi Lines (www.grimaldi-lines.com) runs to/from Civitavecchia (70km from Rome).

By rail. Nowadays you can catch high-speed sleeper services to Barcelona from several European destinations. Renfe-SNCF (www.renfe-sncf.com) and others arrive in Barcelona from cities such as Paris, Milan and Zurich. Trains run four times a day between Barcelona Sants station and Montpellier, where you can connect with the TGV, the French high-speed train. The AVE, the Spanish high-speed train, runs several times a day between Barcelona and Madrid.

RENFE is the Spanish national rail network (www.renfe.com). Local trains in Catalonia, Ferrocarrils Generalitat de Catalunya (FGC; www.fgc.cat), are serviced by the Catalan government.

RENFE honours Interrail, Rail Plus and Eurail cards (the latter sold only outside Europe), and offers discounts to people under 26, senior citizens (over 60) as well as large families.

By car. The highways outside Barcelona are generally excellent. The AP7 motorway leads to Barcelona from France and northern Catalonia; the AP2 connects Barcelona with Madrid, Zaragoza and Bilbao. From Valencia or the Costa del Sol, take the E15 north.

By bus. Several bus companies operate a service to Barcelona, the largest of which is Eurolines (www.eurolines.es). Most arrive at the bus station, Barcelona Nord (tel: 902-260 606), but some run to Barcelona Sants. For more information and schedules, see www.barcelonanord.com.

GUIDES AND TOURS

English-speaking, licensed guides and interpreters may be arranged through the Barcelona Guide Bureau (www.barcelonaguidebureau.com) and The Tour Guy (www.thetourguy.com).

Tours by bus. Barcelona Bus Turístic (www.barcelonabusturistic.cat) offers a tour with three different routes; hop on and off as you please. Two depart from Plaça de Catalunya, one from Port Olímpic from 9am daily; all stops have full timetables. Complete journey time is about two hours, or forty minutes for the Port Olímpic route. Tickets may be purchased online, at Turisme de Barcelona Tourist Information Points, at newspaper kiosks, bookshops and hotels.

On foot. Barcelona Free Walking Tours runs English-speaking guided tours of the Gothic quarter daily at 11am and 3pm. Walks (lasting around two hours) begin at Turisme de Barcelona (Plaça de Catalunya, tel: 622 940 471).

Walks should be booked in advance at a tourist office. Other themed tours are available.

HEALTH AND MEDICAL CARE

Visitors from EU countries are entitled to medical and hospital treatment under the Spanish social security system – you need a European Health Insurance Card (EHIC) or Global Health Insurance Card (GHIC). However, it does not cover everything, and it is advisable to take out private medical insurance. The water is safe to drink, but bottled water is always safest.

In an emergency, head to a main hospital: Hospital Clinic on Villarroel 170 www.hospitalclinic.org); Hospital Dos de Maig on Carrer del Dos de Maig 301 (www.csi.cat). For an ambulance, make your way to an *ambulatorio* (medical centre) or tel: **061**.

Pharmacies *(farmacias)* follow normal business hours but there is generally one in each district that remains open all night and on holidays. The location and phone number of this *farmacia de guardia* is posted on the door of all the others. Tel: **098** for this information.

> Where's the nearest (all-night) pharmacy? **¿Donde está la farmacia (de guardia) más cercana?**
> I need a doctor/dentist **Necesito un médico/dentista**

LGBTQ+ TRAVELLERS

Barcelona has an active queer and gay community and scores of clubs and nightlife options. There's a vibrant LGBTQ+ community, backed up by a supportive city council. Information about the scene – known in Spanish as *el ambiente*, "the atmosphere" – is pretty easy to come by. Sitges, Spain's biggest LGBTQ+ resort, is just forty minutes south of Barcelona by train.

LANGUAGE

Both Catalan *(català)* and Castilian Spanish *(castellano)* are official languages in Catalonia; everyone in Barcelona who speaks Catalan can speak Castilian Spanish but many will not unless absolutely necessary. Street signs are in Catalan. Spanish (Castilian) will get you by, so most of the language tips in this section are given in Spanish.

English – *Catalan* – **Castilian**
Good morning – *Bon dia* – **Buenos días**
Good afternoon – *Bona tarda* – **Buenas tardes**
Goodnight – *Bona nit* – **Buenas noches**
Goodbye – *Adéu* – **Adiós**
Hello – *Hola* – **Hola**
See you later – *Fins desprès* – **Hasta luego**
Please – *Si us plau* – **Por favor**
Thank you – *Gràcies* – **Gracias**
You're welcome – *De res* – **De nada**
Welcome – *Benvinguts* – **Bienvenido**
Do you speak English? – *¿Parla anglés?* – **¿Habla inglés?**
I don't understand. – *No ho entenc* – **No entiendo**
How much is it? – *¿Quant es?* – **¿Cuánto vale?**
Open/closed – *obert/tancat* – **abierto/cerrado**

MONEY

Currency *(moneda)*. The monetary unit of Spain is the euro (symbolised €).

Currency exchange *(cambio)*. Banks and *cajas/caixes* (savings banks) are the best place to exchange currency, offering the best rates with no commission. Banks and exchange offices pay slightly more for travellers' cheques than for cash. Always take your passport when you go to change money. Otherwise, there are several currency exchange spots spread around the city. Rates can fluctuate heavily so pay special attention.

Travellers' cheques *(cheques de viajero)*. Hotels, shops, restaurants and travel agencies may cash travellers' cheques, and so do some banks, where the process is more complicated, but you are likely to get a better rate. You will always need your passport.

Where's the nearest bank/currency exchange office?
¿Dónde está el banco/la casa de cambio más cercana?
I want to change some pounds/dollars **Quiero cambiar
libras/dólares**
Do you accept travellers' cheques? **¿Acceptan cheques de
viajero?**
Can I pay with a credit card? **¿Se puede pagar con tarjeta?**
How much is that? **¿Cuánto es/Cuánto vale?**

OPENING TIMES

Shops. The bigger stores and shopping malls open 10am–9 or 10pm, but smaller shops close in the early afternoon (for lunch).

Banks. Generally open Mon–Fri 8.30am–2pm; in winter also open on Sat 8.30am–1pm.

Government offices and most businesses. Open Mon–Fri 8/9am–2pm and 4–6/7pm. In summer, many businesses work *horas intensivas*, from 8am–3pm, to avoid the hottest part of the day.

Museums. Most Tues–Sat 10am–8pm and Sun 10am–2.30pm. Some close for lunch. Most close on Mondays, with exceptions. Some have later hours in summer on Thursday and Friday, often with bar service.

POLICE

In Barcelona, dial **092** for municipal (city) police and **112** for the autonomous Catalan police. The main police station in the Old Town is at Nou de la Rambla 76–78.

Where's the nearest police station? **¿Dónde está la comisaría
más cercana?**

PUBLIC HOLIDAYS

1 January *Año Nuevo*, New Year's Day

6 January *Epifanía/Los Reyes*, Epiphany

1 May *Fiesta de Trabajo*, Labour Day

23/24 June *Sant Joan*, St Joan's Day

15 August *Asunción*, Assumption

11 September *La Diada*, Catalan National Day

24 September *La Mercè (Mercedes)*, Barcelona's patron saint

1 November *Todos los Santos*, All Saints' Day

6 December *Día de la Constitución*, Constitution Day

8 December *Inmaculada Concepción*, Immaculate Conception

25–26 December *Navidad*, Christmas

MOVABLE DATES

Feb/March *Mardi Gras*, Shrove Tuesday (Carnival)

Late March/April *Viernes Santo*, Good Friday

Late March/April *Lunes de Pascua*, Easter Monday

Mid-June *Corpus Christi*, Corpus Christi

TELEPHONES

Spain's country code is **34**. Barcelona's local area code, **93**, must be dialled before all phone numbers, even for local calls and from abroad (00 34 93 etc.). Frequent callers might consider buying a SIM card for Spain on arrival. The main providers in Spain are Vodafone, Orange, Movistar and Yoigo. To phone the UK from your mobile dial 00 (+) 44 and the number, omitting the first 0.

TIME ZONES

Spanish time is the same as that in most of Western Europe – Greenwich Mean Time plus one hour. Clocks go forward one hour in spring and back one hour in autumn, so Spain is generally one hour ahead of London.

TIPPING

Since a service charge is normally included on hotel and restaurant bills, tipping is not obligatory but it's usual to leave small change (about 5 percent of the bill) on a bar counter, and 5–10 percent on restaurant bills.

TOILETS

Toilet doors are distinguished in Catalan by an 'H' for *homes* (men) or 'D' for *dones* (women).

Where are the toilets? **¿Dónde están los servicios?**

TOURIST INFORMATION

Barcelona tourist offices. The main tourist office is Turisme de Barcelona, Plaça de Catalunya 17, below street level (www.barcelonaturisme.com), open daily 8.30am–9.00pm. Informació Turística de Catalunya in Palau Robert, Passeig de Gràcia 107 (www.gencat.cat), provides information about Catalonia. There are also offices at Sants Station, the airport and on Plaça del Portal de la Pau.

TRANSPORT

Getting around town is easy, rapid and inexpensive. Transport information: www.tmb.cat or www.renfe.com.

By metro. The metro (twww.tmb.cat) is the fastest and easiest way to navigate the city. Stations are marked by a red diamond symbol. The metro runs Mon–Thurs, Sun and holidays 5am–midnight, Fri 5am–2am, Sat 24 hours.

By bus (autobús). Barcelona buses (www.tmb.cat) have routes and hours clearly marked at the stops. Buses run daily 4.25am–11pm (variable depending on route), with infrequent night services from 10.40pm to 5am.

The official Tourist Bus, which passes numerous interesting sights in the city is excellent; you can jump on and off at any stop (see page 133). An air-conditioned bus, rather unfortunately called the 'Tomb Bus', runs during business hours from the Plaça de Catalunya to the uptown Plaça Pius XII, covering all the smart shopping areas.

By train. FGC (www.fgc.cat) trains are useful for reaching Barcelona's upper neighbourhoods Sarrià, Pedralbes and Tibidabo, the Parc de Collserola behind Tibidabo and nearby towns such as Sant Cugat, Terrassa and

Sabadell. These depart from Plaça de Catalunya. The FGC trains also run from Plaça Espanya to Montserrat, Colònia Güell and other destinations.

Tickets. You can buy a single ticket from the driver on buses, or a multiple card (*tarjeta multi-viaje T10*), which is punched once you are inside the bus or in an automatic machine as you enter the station. This is valid for bus, metro and urban FGC lines and allows transfer from one means of transport to the other with no extra charge, within a time limit. It works out at nearly half the price of the equivalent in single tickets. Buy the T10 at stations, banks or *estancs*. The T10 can also be used on RENFE trains within Zone 1, which includes the airport (but it's not valid on the metro line connecting the airport with the city).

When's the next bus/train to…? **¿Cuándo sale el próximo autobús/tren para…?**
bus station **estación de autobuses**
A ticket to… **Un billete para…**
single (one-way) **ida**
return (round-trip) **ida y vuelta**
How much is the fare to…? **¿Cuánto es la tarifa a …?**

By taxi. Taxi apps Uber and FREENOW have the largest fleet available, and are relatively inexpensive. Black-and-yellow taxis are metered, with a supplementary charge added at the end of the journey.

VISAS AND ENTRY REQUIREMENTS

Members of EU countries need only a passport. Visas are needed by non-EU nationals unless their country has a reciprocal agreement with Spain.

Barcelona Transport

Sant Cugat, Sabadell & Terrassa

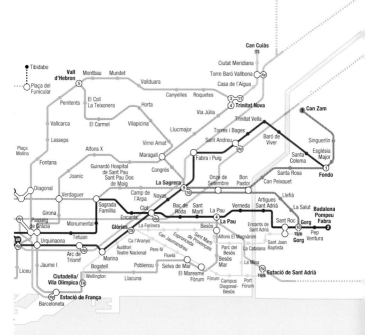

Mar Mediterrània

THE **MINI** ROUGH GUIDE TO
BARCELONA

First Edition 2025

Editor: Joanna Reeves
Author: Neil Schlecht
Updater: Justin McDonnell
Picture Editor: Piotr Kala
Picture Manager: Tom Smyth
Cartography Update: Katie Bennett
Production Operations Manager: Katie Bennett
Publishing Technology Manager: Rebeka Davies
Head of Publishing: Sarah Clark
Photography Credits: All images Shutterstock except: Corrie Wingate/Apa Publications 12, 14MC, 14TC, 1ST, 15M, 16TL, 16ML, 33, 34, 39, 42, 44, 46, 52, 56, 67, 68, 71, 72, 73, 75, 78, 81, 83, 89, 102; Dreamstime.com 91; Greg Gladman/Apa Publications 24, 94, 114; Gregory Wrona/Apa Publications 48; Gure Gipuzkoa 28; iStock 14TL, 66, 87, 99; Public domain 22, 26
Cover Credits: Park Guell **iStock**

About the author

Justin McDonnell is a London-based travel writer whose work has appeared in UK and US publications like Thrillist, Atlas Obscura and Lonely Planet. Over the past decade, he's lived in and written about Croatia (as editor of Time Out Croatia), Spain, Slovenia, Italy and the UK. Most recently, he's contributed to The Rough Guide to Slow Travel in Europe, Mini Rough Guide Bologna, Rough Guides Walks and Tours: Barcelona and Time Out London for Londoners.

Distribution

UK, Ireland and Europe: Apa Publications (UK) Ltd; sales@roughguides.com
United States and Canada: Ingram Publisher Services; ips@ingramcontent.com
Australia and New Zealand: Booktopia; retailer@booktopia.com.au
Worldwide: Apa Publications (UK) Ltd; sales@roughguides.com

Special Sales, Content Licensing and CoPublishing

Rough Guides can be purchased in bulk quantities at discounted prices. We can create special editions, personalised jackets and corporate imprints tailored to your needs. sales@roughguides.com; http://roughguides.com

All Rights Reserved
© 2025 Apa Digital AG
License edition © Apa Publications Ltd UK

Printed in Czech Republic

This book was produced using **Typefi** automated publishing software.

No part of this book may be reproduced, stored in a retrieval system or transmitted in any form or means electronic, mechanical, photocopying, recording or otherwise, without prior written permission from Apa Publications.

Contact us

Every effort has been made to provide accurate information in this publication, but changes are inevitable. The publisher cannot be held responsible for any resulting loss, inconvenience or injury sustained by any traveller as a result of information or advice contained in the guide. We would appreciate it if readers would call our attention to any errors or outdated information, or if you feel we've left something out. Please send your comments with the subject line "Rough Guide Mini Barcelona Update" to mail@uk.roughguides.com.